Penguin Modern Poe
VOLUME 10

Douglas Oliver, born 1937, has published two novels, research into prosody and eight books of poetry, most recently a volume of *Selected Poems* in the United States and his New York satire, *Penniless Politics* (Bloodaxe). After thirteen years of journalism in England and France, he attended Essex University, and became a university lecturer and freelance writer. He lived in New York for five years, is married to the American poet Alice Notley, and now teaches at the British Institute in Paris.

Denise Riley was born in Carlisle in 1948. She lives in London with her three children, and teaches at Goldsmiths' College. Her doctorate was in philosophy. She has also worked in intellectual history, in Britain and America, and was writer-in-residence at the Tate Gallery, London, in 1996. Her prose books are *War in the Nursery* (Virago, 1983) and '*Am I that Name?*' (Macmillan, 1988), and she edited *Poets on Writing* (Macmillan, 1992). Poetry collections include *Dry Air* (Virago, 1985) and *Mop Mop Georgette, New and Selected Poems 1986–1993* (Reality Street Editions, 1993).

Iain Sinclair was born in Cardiff in 1943. He has been a documentary film-maker, publisher of Albion Village Press and 'used' book-dealer. His poetry collections include *Lud Heat* (1975), *Suicide Bridge* (1979), *Flesh Eggs & Scalp Metal: Selected Poems 1970–1987* (1989) *Jack Elam's Other Eye (1991),* and he edited *Conductors of Chaos* (Picador, 1996), an anthology of contemporary poetry. His novels are *White Chappell, Scarlet Tracings* (1987), *Downriver* (1991), which won the James Tait Black Memorial Prize, and *Radon Daughters* (1994). He lives in east London.

The Penguin Modern Poets Series

Penguin Modern Poets

VOLUME 10

DOUGLAS OLIVER

DENISE RILEY

IAIN SINCLAIR

PENGUIN BOOKS

Published by the Penguin Group
Penguin Books Ltd, 27 Wrights Lane, London w8 5tz, England
Penguin Books USA Inc., 375 Hudson Street, New York, New York 10014, USA
Penguin Books Australia Ltd, Ringwood, Victoria, Australia
Penguin Books Canada Ltd, 10 Alcorn Avenue, Toronto, Ontario, Canada m4v 3b2
Penguin Books (NZ) Ltd, 182–190 Wairau Road, Auckland 10, New Zealand

Penguin Books Ltd, Registered Offices: Harmondsworth, Middlesex, England

This selection first published 1996
10 9 8 7 6 5 4 3 2 1

Typeset in 10.5/14pt Monotype Garamond
Rowland Phototypesetting Ltd, Bury St Edmunds, Suffolk
Printed in England by Clays Ltd, St Ives plc

Contents

Douglas Oliver

Our Family is Full of Problems

A long, easy line of introduction, as if I'm a poet prosing
    alongside you,
a stranger, half-turning in his enthusiasms. We're in England,
descending the house-combed hillsides of Coventry,
early seventies, when the idea for these poems was born;
and we enter the shattered Hillfields suburb under the ring
    road.
I show you the surviving top shops,
terraces with wide upper windows blank in dark brick
where once the ribbon weavers' looms throbbed, driven
by a long, easy belt drive through attics of these joined homes
from one combustion engine in the end garden. Came the
    fall of cotton.
Came Second World War bombs, came socialist planners
bulldozing Hillfields, came the acrid fires of the homeless
on rubbled sites beside high rises which trapped infants
in sweating flats far from their natural earth, families
    collapsing,
some crime – much exaggerated, some prostitution – from
    outside.
Came courage to live through a city's class and racial tensions,
scapegoats in 'Coventry's Square Mile of Crime'.
Now came the government again, with a full purse, to restore
the vanished community, as if money could replace the
    granny in 25
or the old man who played the spoons in 28, or the larger
    family

2

that was once the suburb of Hillfields. I turn to you, as if
   newly excited,
to explain how those planners implanted community centres,
went for mixed housing, sought to make a sunrise in the
   slums.
And created a middle-class boom instead. See the problem
   families
scatter as the suburb goes bourgeois. I point to the smart
   new brick.
See the hard truth of it: a free-market nation will stick such
   families
right at the bottom; they'll never afford a house even one
   rung
above lowest and slip modestly aside from new building plots
into the next meanest doorway.

This relaxed walking – not a singing – gives us time for
   specifics;
but to see the problems of families puts a chord string of
   iron in the heart,
still there many years later in a country obsessed with free
   markets,
following the gleam of international power blocs, the EU,
   the WTO.
And I read a *Daily Mail* economist forecasting great wealth
for all free-market countries. 'Of course, there will be basket
   cases,
such as Africa.' And I grab you by the arm.
'Did you hear that? Africa! Not a Coventry suburb, a whole
   continent
written off in our free-trade fanaticism.' As if
holding your arm I face towards Africa and write these poems
as representative of a failed British imagination.

The iron chord is struck and I walk with you in Dar es
   Salaam.
In golden light move the stereotype dark suits
of World Bankers, planning, funding, organizing,
   implementing,
evaluating corrugated sheets of shanties rattling in the sunny
   wind.
The government, lenient on forced eviction, has targeted
these slums for upgrading with World Bank funding
still in these early seventies; it will allocate building plots,
   slap down
fully-serviced cement foundations for squatters, a housing
   bank for loans,
providing you build to old colonial standards.
Low-income earners, the self-employed, the jobless
can't get these loans, can't build to such standards,
and the Hillfields, Coventry, story repeats itself.
The poor move out to new marginal, unserviced
   squatterdoms.
I follow them in my imagination and imagine I am following
the old slum-dwellers of Hillfields in Coventry
inexorably moving on.
Come the petit bourgeois, the middle classes,
come the slippery deals in land, till even the Bank admits:
'It is believed that many of the plots have unofficially
transferred to more affluent individuals.'
An inner city opened up to free-market forces
will scatter the poor. World trade agreements blindly
   following
the forces that created a Hillfields are creating an Africa
ever falling behind this financial neo-colonialism,
the World Bank credo, the credo of the GATT, to help an
   Africa

bulldozed already by its own politicians.

Then I take your arm again and remark, 'I have risked prose, a walking measure, to explain why I've written these poems.'

The Unseeing Drum

If I drummed on the long Dahomey tambour,
I'd be bumbling, blind in ludicrous Western clothes,
that tambour's wooden tubes stepped at the foot
like a half-closed sea captain's telescope; I'd be

drumming of old things I can half see: of bamboo-
stilted houses elongated by water reflections
as if I were paddling to the floating market of Ganvié
while fishermen cast nets in jelly-fish patterns.

So, almost, I drum on the Dahomey tambour.
My hands can't make me see, and I haven't looked
at Mali's thatched houses, the mud rain-washed off
walls ribbed by uncooked bricks poking through.

Or I put Soukous music into my ears from Zaire
and watch pesticide machines huff injections
into a Kinshasa sewer; a woman's hut in Topoke holds
two bamboo beds, food bowls on a stick-legged shelf.

Tapping blindly in rhythm on my work-table,
I see women across Africa stoop to chipped bowls
of peanuts and they grunt at their labour, the body rocking,
scale-arm burdened by the cupped hand's loveliness.

With my hands tapping perhaps without sanctity
as on taut antelope skin, I glimpse wooden shanties
in Nouakchott, corridors of all doors, black-
swathed mothers holding babies with two hair clumps

on their shaven heads, one at the front, one at the back.
Unseeing, I must yet see, boat-making in Niger

where a steel bar burns potholes in wood slabs and the thin
pirogue spreads out like crocodile-chewed nougat.

The women are off to market, millet stalks on oxen:
swaggering on camels is reserved for the men.
The children scoop pits in sand, playing Marella
– or tic-tac-toe. Half blinded by the male sun,

the boys dream of being horsemen. In Uganda
other children learn shopping, sugar cane, gourds,
for merchandise; muzzled camels gloom by a sidewalk
hat souk in Libya, coned pots with cockerel tails.

Structural beams spike from baked earth mosques
in Burkina Faso, a palm trunk with flute-holes makes
a village ladder, woman climbing, hand reaching
for grain and fruit to dry on the roof of her house.

Skate fish flap down into Sahel sand, gasp,
and become dark tents; a Guinea woman's hair
is the shape of a seal's head; by the gushing springs
of Chaouen black robes float over sparkling cobblestones.

Elsewhere, money and talent whisper their telepathy
in coastal capitals, yet everywhere as names flash by
in my drumming women appear, washing clothes
under river bridges, *un amour* shadowed on the bankside.

Sunlight glares down those city avenues where blurred
humans hurry into their potential for richness:
in Conakry, pineapples enter a factory chunker;
Moroccan biologists work in impossible snowfalls

of cotton branches to improve yields; alluvial gold
is panned in Ilesha; a hand pours libations
into chemical pipettes in Lagos; it was Barclays put
an ugly wafer-biscuit bank on those oily streets.

White blocks front the Zanzibar straits of Tanzania,
where the canoe's striped sail bounds out on its ropes,
fishing boats tug at the men launching them,
hulls leap in surf, and the flying water is the pleasure.

I ask you, 'Pretend to have sight a moment, for the sun
under our lids will warm us.' A real blind drummer
from the animist Dogon in Mali taps on the skin
with curved stick, seeing all that I don't see, and I see him.

The Borrowed Bow

The moment stings, shorting like an old wireless
of bakelite body with a trellised raffia screen.
The shadowy corner's acrid with electricity,
blue air frazzed with black
in a cliffside house blank-windowed towards France.
But around the space of shock are other rooms
where old men, sitting by their wirelesses,
wear country check worsteds with a fleck of red
blodged with gravy. This moment
is a vanishing point on a post-war seacoast,
the pier blown up in case of German invasion.

The rooms still have that slow life
moving in them, a termite-gnawed Asante mask
on the walls of a retired colonial official,
an assegai from elsewhere in Africa,
a boot-polish shield, a bow, a poisoned arrow;
for there's an unexplored magic in all time,
a survival even now of a toothless mouth
sopping at a biscuit, a hand trembling
on a bony knee, about to reach
for porcelain on a frame of swivelling trays,
thin finger crooked as for a trigger.

I borrowed the bow of black hardwood,
took it and a bamboo stick into the garden.
Couldn't pull the leather string back;
the magic of the bow-spar wouldn't bend for me.
I knew I was just meddling. So I went indoors
to fiddle with the wireless innards:

electronic emotions and jerky excitements
in the village of valves, which cracked like gunfire,
a tracer arc streaked across dusty connections,
as if before the snap of it, the coil of smoke,
a tiny bow had shot a brilliant arrow.

The King's Garden

In old Bulawayo was a king's garden –
Lobengula's, son of Mzilikazi
who came from forests of Ngome
and founded the Matabele people.
Some garden!
A bamboo stockade floored with maggoty dung
grazed by hundreds of sheep and goats.
Lobengula sat on a block of wood,
a huge man, smiling, worried, friendly,
cruel in the laws of the tribe.
Around him 30 whites, wanting to mine
legendary gold, scrabbling for treaties,
mistranslated for the illiterate king
by the smooth missionary Helm
whom Cecil Rhodes was paying well.
Three other envoys of Rhodes
squatted on haunches in the dung.
The dapper London lawyer Maguire,
MP, Fellow of All Souls, stuck
out a leg to raise his buttocks from the mire.
A chorus greeted this discourtesy.
'Gh-h-o,' called the younger warriors gleefully.
'He wants to be as big as the king.'
The king of the Matabele,
Lobengula, sat on his wood block, smiling.

An official from the Rhodes mines
in Kimberley, one Thompson,
muttered aside to Maguire: 'It's as much
as your life's worth to shirk homage.'

Down squatted Maguire, back into dung,
down squatted Charles Dunnel Rudd,
and it was managed like that,
the Rudd Concession,
born in the filth of false homage.
The king's most trusted white friend,
a son of the great missionary Moffat,
spoke in his ear (but secretly for Rhodes).
The king, tricked about the treaty's words,
and thinking of a few small mining holes,
signed away his country.
Better advised, he panicked, sent
envoys to the white Queen, proclaiming,
'Lobengula did not say these words,'
(for land couldn't be owned in private).
Unthinkable to the king a queen could lie.
Victoria wrote a warning letter
in the Africans-speak-English language:
'A King gives a stranger an ox,
not his whole herd –
beware in placing your trust.'
Her messenger, Maund, in league with Rhodes,
quietly lost this letter,
and men in high places
returned the envoys roundabout
to the king via South America,
while Rhodes finagled his Royal Charter,
an excuse for the Charter Ro law
of the sjambok and of the Maxim gun
mounted within the king's kraal,
its tripod spiked into the dung.
Yes, it was managed like that,
an excuse for wholesale invasion,

seizure of the king's maggoty garden,
slaughter of the Matabele peoples
as they fled the Bulawayo kraal.
And there was hardly any gold.
The treaty men simply settled the land.

We British of a third generation
have seen this treachery playing out
down dishonourable decades, until –
Matabele and Mashona fighting back –
colonials retired, disgruntled,
to our childhood suburb. Sometimes
a garden we stopped at:
quite manic with
its lawn of absolute green. Triangles
and crescents for flower beds held
brick-orange lumps of marigolds
and bruised-yellow pansies in military lines,
an exact border of daffodils,
blooded by tulips, green budding red,
like laughter turned tubercular.
The ancient captain behind panes of glass
in clover-shaped concrete mouldings
glowered as we wondered why
his mind delighted in these rows of bulls'-eyes,
grass edges moustache-clipped,
beauty so tight-chested
that it gave a harsh cough,
opened its windows at us,
and ordered small boys to clear off,
go to the cliffs, get away from the iron gate.

The Infibulation Ceremony

We have reached the limit of poetry: Western people's ignorance of
how their own cultures are viewed by traditionalist societies is too
profound. The following poem could never be read in illiterate deserts.
Like Alice Walker and Pratibha Parmar working in West Africa, you
could make a courageous film on the subject of infibulation. Failing
that, a poem might yet become a sort of film shot from a distance, an
attempt to project on to the air, via a beam of good wishes, an imagined
ceremony for the sake of young girls who are infibulated without ceremony by nomad Somalians, almost on the move.

A Jeep, its shock absorbers gone, thumps
across pocks in the level desert scrub
faster than the black-faced sheep with fat tails
prodded onwards by the nomad women.

If we have time and water
we stop and let the clan drink;
if we have neither we drive on
inventing our film about infibulation.

We drive up to a low escarpment
and look down on a hollow littered with people,
livestock scattered among the rocky slopes
by a well cairned with boulders.

Near this home well on their April journey
the women dismantle the hut sticks
from the ship slew of camel humps,
setting up Nissen huts of mats and skins.

Herded then by a man, disburdened
camels sigh and settle down

in the rubbled hollow of the home well
in the northern Somali Republic.

Off to the side – we swivel the camera –
where thorns are piled for the fence
the nomads are busy at their camp
fastening the huts with bark ropes.

One little hut that's new
arrived on the coarse grass from the sky.
It's the virgin spirit placed there somehow,
dazzling the nomads with the sunshine on it.

They sew up its door flaps with the ropes
so no man may crawl through
a tiny slit left at the bottom
like a button-hole in a missing shirt

Then on dry highlands of Somalia
we set their young girls to go dancing
in virginity round the sutured hut:
this is their sorrow in private places.

They dance in a hurt, stiff motion,
stick-legged as if avoiding stones
blood gleaming on brown thighs
tears in expressionless eyes.

The mouths of these children are silenced
by tradition: that they be made clean,
that they not become promiscuous,
that they be desirable for marriage

with a sewn vagina, stripped of pleasure,
crossed with thorns, as if the surgeons
had sutured the mouth of a healthy baby
leaving the palette uselessly cleft.

But this film is fantasy imagined from books
and my inability to suffer the thorns
that make religions stand erect, or that make
a temple's entrance so narrow.

We shoot the girls from a distance, telephoto,
forgetting the funds we raised in Britain,
forgetting the clan-lords warring in Mogadishu,
forgetting the entrenchment of Islam

into hard-line law, here called Shafi'i;
while the West threatens Islam with bombs
or rich products bearing our labels,
may our Jeeps not insult their culture.

We know these illiterates will never see our film;
so will the children make their children dance
that queer dance in this cinema-wilderness?
Our Jeep moves on, its tracks soon blown over.

The film is more penetrant than propaganda;
for it shows the silence here;
and the thorny look in the girls' eyes;
it shows the male wind, harsh, hot.

(Dancing and film imagery influenced by Alice Walker and Pratibha
Parmar, *Warrior Marks: Female Genital Mutilation and the Sexual Blinding of
Women*, Harcourt Brace & Co., New York, 1993.)

16

The Childhood Map

An Africa the size of a British park
cracked like a white map,
a manageable terrain,
or coloured in with adventures
for boyhood dreams of the bush,
brown and sere, gazelles,
scouted by cheetahs on their hills,
streaming over the high plateaux
of Kenya beneath the fuselage
of a plane that lands long ago, lightly,
into history. In present time
it could only land tourists,
and it's worse than that.

Locust aircraft turns on its wire arm
lands in a toyshop window. Trembles.
Child minds excited but blank.
As adults, we are reading
liberal history books:
the oily tones of the Whitehall elite
with their city interests and ties
setting up Kikuyu Home Guards
to fight Kikuyu Mau Mau.
For every white man killed
four hundred Africans killed.

Toy planes still landing long ago.
Kenya gripped by one-party rule now
or two-party, uneasily.
If Britain were beset by famines,

would it be governable?
Shining pupils of our aristocratic schools
rise to well-fed pomposity
of managing nations
of making the EU competitive
against boys running ragged
down river banks in Nairobi.

The toyshop window lights up again.
A slender plane with medicaments
or is it a white human body
is flying low over Africa dispensing
a fraction of Western money spent on AIDS:
HIV truck drivers in Rwanda
say, 51 per cent; Uganda
36 per cent; Kenya who
knows, 19 per cent; commercial
sex workers in bars
34 to 88 per cent –

the stanza
breaks apart, Africa
cracks like a painted tin landscape
in a child's small attention.
Elsewhere beyond this window
its greatness breathes like a leopard.
Will these statistics never be finished?
Can we never get on the right side of them?
Watching our little plane
on its slender piece of wire
land behind the window.

The New Medicine

'Three leading London hospitals have completed all routine treatments that the authorities had provided for that year.'

Hospitals too productive, come to the end of their budgets for ops,
routine surgery halted till the next budget, way of the world would mean
some bag lady didn't get her op, the bishop got his
with medical insurance like all higher-ups
on the internal market for organ repair.
Bank clerk not pushy, only a gristly testicular tumour, probably not him,
wasn't he nearly sixty, had to wait for a specialist, no big problem,
actress got her ovary op and a lot of attention in the media, bank clerk
    who?
He didn't die, you know, not him, these are not sentimental matters but
    bred in
the bone morals that what we do is sacred to each other, fat
chance. Baby mine, in memory, covered blue-black with staff infection,
nurses dabbing with calomine lotion, joking the sweetest jokes,
as the black invaded your neck.
What if those nurses had been infected by profit?
We have the money, you know, no problem. Baby, in memory still,
writhed on the bed, skin of a certain mottling, dried mackerel skin.
What if the baby ran into debt?
Should have looked where they were running when they voted for the
    bastards, half a nation.
My mother voted for them, didn't look, had a mastectomy one time
but laughed when I said she had one breast in the grave now, and
medical insurance,
took an aneurism later, very cheery woman,
cheery being almost the highest moral gift because it beams outwards.

Price plays a part when the State chooses your hospital
no one gets the best without paying.
Nurse came to you, mother, like my conscience,
cool and neutral, warm and smiley, not like my restless individualism;
she built your body up in bed like a cornucopia riddled with it,
    conscience.
Have you had your medicine, man? said she to mother,
and I think of African lands where illness was a communal fault,
and witch doctors beat out psychiatrists in curing neuroses.
Oh but Britain's our medicine man, dying of its own accord.
Sometimes there's nothing to lift the heart from the death bed.
No grand causes left to fight for, said Osborne's old play.
But that's when the one cause becomes huge and obvious,
seen in the amused astral focus of the death principle:
our lives no more important than our deaths,
but by god you'd better get them both right on line,
no jumping the queue to live,
no pushing others forward in the queue to die.

NEW YORK / PARIS POEMS

A Parable of Good Government

A spiritual Mayoress in perfect mind proposes
that all remembered cities be one city of wax.

The walls last for one act of her fine government
ever reborn in the matrix of her absolute goodwill.

Let them appear again, the streets of wax sarcophagi,
low walls of houses rising, honeycombing acres.

In the instant workmanship of this mind-moulding
within seconds you see town hall vistas

past cereous porticos of churches; and terraces
with doors crude still, gouged like pigeons' nostrils

into façades becoming vertical. Overhead, those
motorways will never be firm enough for vehicles.

For some moments you have a stretch of lifetime
to lean against slippery walls, peer into alleys

where brownish dusk drifts with purple-grained dust
in the smoky smell of the mind's making.

The deadened streets have no time to fill up with crowds
but you can find magnanimous hints of citizens

in graffiti carved into soft walls saying
'I want no vengeance and will forebear my envy.'

The city melts already, candle flames spurt
on battlements whose age is measured in moments.

Yet there's time to see not views but a view
of the whole of your life spent in cities.

Doves with waxy beaks settle round St Paul's rotundas
Parisian boulevards look encaustic against blue sky.

All holds trembling like a line from *The Merchant of Venice*
which passes the lips sweetly but stays in air:

>   'Look how the floor of heaven
> is thick inlaid with patens of bright gold.'

This parable written in New York, its present malleable
only through lower development taxes, ousting the poor.

The Heron

I talk of voices either real or virtual in my ear;
of shadows, only those that pass over islands' sunny turf
vivid to my eye. But when I come to all my birds,
all I've ever seen, they are too many. I talk of things unseen.

Together, they would pack the sky like moving embroidery
in the white silks, browns and blacks of their great tribe,
like endless litters of puppies writhing,
a heavenly roof alive but no progress of flight in it.

Every memory adds to this intricate plot;
starting up redshanks first, and they bank, flashing white,
across a sepia estuary where I felt freedom
in watching their undulating patterns on the air.

They flight down but hold at mid-height: horizontal
stick puppets of the Styx. The black light whitens
with the harmonious wings of swan formations,
the day cast over with their bright feathering.

Behind the swans the sky absolutely fills with starlings
homing to roost as once I saw them over Stonehenge;
gulls flock up and hold there, and brown passeriformes
spring between airspaces and stop on invisible branches.

Millions of birds, crows and daws, teal,
quicker wing-beated than wigeon, among mallard hordes;
swifts print arrows on the pulsating featheriness;
the sky is covered over with the puppy litters.

I can't tell you all the names; I'm worried
about the birds rabbling the sky. D'you suppose
I can avoid even the dusty body of every sparrow,
or every sparrow hawk flipping over a thicket?

Unseen, this nature crowds my mind. If there's pulsation,
it's disturbing; if stasis it's a painting
and all the life goes out; but any sudden switch
between pulse and the static is schizophrenic.

In the foreground of the multifarious flights
one talismanic bird, a heron, lifts to the top
of its single leg and takes off like an umbrella.
Fluff in a corner of the past becomes grey flame.

Its shoulders unshackle and heave, legs become the
    addendum,
the beak stabs out purposefully from the sunken neck.
It sails. In this flight's brevity
I find what lives for me among all the dead songs.

Taking Stock of Woods

Grey cloud roof sliding backwards lifts blue sky
into the notch between hill-lines green au gratin.
Pom-pommed, the slopes barge trees into valley turbulence.
Along the summits, sunlit topknots,
down to mid-distance, puffs, explosions, uprisings,
striking tall, and achieved stature, horizontal shadow-flows
running along the sides, mists of green dreaming
scabbed with blackened precipices, as if the hills
were green dogs with the mange. The new sky
now lightly creamed with softened stratus settles out.

Near at hand fast river speeds under the tickety sun leaves
river swirls under wallowing beech shades,
something in sliding of flow-speed under fragmented stirring.

In front, then, these near woods; behind, the hilly woods
and green freckles on the blue simple sky.
Wilderness valley grazed as by sheep by tree tops.

Seeing holds lazily in union, or the eye keeps particularizing:
across stream, a green infanta hawthorn in a clearing,
another dwarfed and crazy as a green Jack Frost.
Insect thin trees, lion mane one
whose lower branches show hands sunlit from windows.
As many shapes as among shifting clouds:
fists and sparklers and flingers and fleurs-de-lis
and candles and fans and umbrella spokes
and florid gestures and controlled
and upstands and seal-heads of them
and black scribble branches and cauliflower tightness
above trunks in perspectives changing.

Sunlight splats dead leaves, or its pools calm, widening,
under ivy-wrapped sticks and angry
crossings out and quiet acceptance of variance,
inter-breed decorum and dashed away sketches
and spears against shields
and scilla and anemone shapes and fringes,
witchfingers and a competition of heights
and sudden dark success in silhouette and watch trees
and bird releasers and
denuded, bottom-heavy trees whose skirts
have slid to their ankles
or those top-crowded with skirts stuck over their heads;
also a matron, by which is meant the elegance
of mysterious limbs imagined by small boys
under the full skirt of a stately aunt;
and overblown and undershot and roundly frisky
and up and down gents and side to side wiggers
and hands signing briskly and stickety.

Among all those well plumaged trees over there,
another blackened carcase with its claws' grab,
and branches kebabbed with irregular leaf clumps.

The clearing comes close in a magnifying lens,
its forms protozoic or fronded in flat clear water,
under-pool browns rotted and furred by acid rains.
Beside it, a yes-no probability tree of geometric branches
and spotted and starred with leaf splodge on bark,
trees deformed into ugly questions,
and the all-decorative lacking solid base,
the 'pretty girls' of it
and proffered argument or arm, and intimate in scale,
or distant, and matted with light like grimed hair locks
and frizzy-ribbed and blackcocked and turkey-necked branches

with odd-clumped leaves like wattles,
masses underbellied in shadows,
or brusque and crimson-brown,
and each in conversation for to share the light,
not a squabble but a metaphysical shouldering into spaces
slowly across time.

The trees offer you blossoms like meringues
on an angled tray.

Sap green, veridian, emerald, grass green,
golf-course green, park green, sea green,
apple green, chartreuse, evergreen,
sparrow green, mallard green, greenshank green,
bird-limed leaves,
algae green, gutter green, drain green,
iron green, teeth green, blossoms green as teeth,
stem green, reed tops greeny-grey,
dawn-sky green, storm green,
old boat paint green, old post green,
seaweed green, tide mark on wood green,
green straw, blazer green,
and Holy Grail green, and Green Man green,
and Green Party green,
well, vote for it, vote for the green,
and white of day confusing now the blue sky.

The Soul as Crumpled Bedsheet

Moon shoots into fumy night sky,
worn down coin in fulgurous green,
as we arrive at Tompkins Square Park
after hotly debating a medieval sermon
at Sheila's house: has the soul a pure core
and a penumbra of ideas through which alone
the shadowy events of every day
come nearer the disc's intense white centre?

We go in, to watch *Star Trek*'s portentous
races against time: a scientist
looks at his daughter's soil samples –
their planet is dying; oh yes, their love is pure,
as pure as I'd wish the daughter-love to be
in a Britain from which I'm self-exiled.
This is the night of the eclipse:
by 12.30 a thumb print blurs half the moon,
and something restless and unachieved
follows me through sleep.

The roar of the garbage truck wakes me up
and releases through my window screen
the ill smell of the weekend on St Mark's Place
like a distillation of sweet-foul bodily corruption
around the perimeter of the untarnished soul,
as that haunting medieval language says.
One side of the bedsheet's rumpled
by my writhing last night. Your sheet, under you,
is a broad lath or a smoothed stream

in your peace last night and again this morning
within the whorls of our anxious river.

My back is stiff; it's urgent to pee.
I crawl down the bed, wagging my naked ass,
over a deep blue mohair blanket,
so that if you opened your eyes
my hot core asshole would be seen
by the cool core of your soul.
From the bathroom I turn aside
to my stepson's soiled green armchair,
an hour to go before I make coffee.
He's away in Europe; so I can sit down
to read *Religion and the Decline of Magic* –
when I remember I was dreaming of an Elizabethan
child's translucent face contorted in sorrow
at the absence of her father.

The Jains and the Boxer

I

The Jain monk would live in unending harmlessness,
shedding karma, confessing, studying for the fasting death.
He avoids quarrels and politics,
may not repair three unmended garments, nuns four,
has rayaharana, the hand broom of wool or grass,
to clear living things from his path,
a cloth to wipe animate dust from his face

and to prevent such beings entering mouth or nose.
He takes care not to walk too far after rain
because life springs up abundantly then
and must not be damaged.
At dawn, he examines utensils and his skin
to preserve tiny souls;
he will not wash limbs, treat wounds or eczema,
may spend hours in immobility save
for involuntary breathing, coughing and physical secreting.
The monk's presence may be scarcely bearable:
the filth (mala) on the acarya Hemacandra
brought his sect the honorary name of Maladharin.
We find such things in the Cheyasutta Mahanisiha,
whose Salluddharana explains contrition and confession;
and whose Kammavivagavivarana
encourages chastity, warns of sexuality and aggressive evils.

II

The boxer imposes 100 per cent will
punching harm into harm in sadistic rhythms.
He's called Alan Boum Boum Minter, Mo Hope,
Rocky This, Kid or Killer That.
His history comes in puffs and spurts.
Listen to the bollocky tights, buttocky satins
of Bob Fitzimmons in his longjohns.
Since then, all the boxers have fallen,
broken-legged spiders,
Joe Gans 'in his famous fighting pose'
'the old master', said the great Fleischer,
fallen. Patterson's head down
arms wide on the floor,
all fire out, while Johansson
waits in the corner like a fire hydrant.

Straight nose punches.
The Woodcock straight left
Cribb's face a creased bun
his left staggering Molyneux
Teddy Baldock leaning back but flattening Kid Pattenden's
    nose.
Bombardier Billy Wells straight on to Porky Flynn's jaw.
The closed socket of old timers, badly drawn,
like the head of a fleshy screw,
a caterpillar trickling down the cheek of Marciano
craze marks on Mills's eye v. Baksi
but you should see the Eskimo eye
of Lesnevich, head in towels, K.O.
over Mills, 10 rounds, May 1946.
Blotches on the imperfectly inked glyph of Pruden
Walcott's face bringing its forehead crumbling down
in the 'Moment of No Return', said *The Ring*.
Treacle round the eye of Cruz
then the crudding round that of Ramos
Chuvalo's face blind, blown,
but that wasn't the bloodiest fight ever known;
some would say 'Harlem' Tommy Murphy
bombing out Abe Attell
the face of Attell covered in shoeblack
imagine that the black is red
just the fixation on red
Pone Kingpetch dethrones Perez
despite a clown's eye made up bloodily
Cooper's eye versus Clay/Ali
the face so grey against the shattered crevice
the light of the game extinguished, turning liquid,
gradually the blood is spent

hollow sockets of 'The Pugilist', bronze,
in the National Museum of Rome.

III

The boxer's sounds interrupt plosively,
while the Jaina vibrate, so repetitive in consonant
that all is almost vowel, a continuous voicing.
We wish for that passivity, the single vowel of wonder,
unchanging reverence for the sacred. But we fall
into Frenchified voodoo sacrifice: the clean blow,
sudden slice at a cockerel neck. It's disgusting
to gain erotic victory at such a price.
The Jains know the flow of time free of harm.
The boxer knows its beat: destruction and renewal.
Poetic music flows, undulates, hits beats.

Well of Sorrows in Purple Tinctures

These thoughts in purple knots of cloud
dash down false lightning flashes like
neon signs above the glistening
Grands Boulevards, illuminating streetwise
melodramas not without beauty when
the will grows weary of the nightlong life
and you go walking.

I keep returning to Paris from scenes of death;
each time a problem with the plumbing

lets out the teary waters.
Plumber came to plumb my flat
on the rue des Messageries just now,
disjointed the pipes behind the bath tiles,
refilled the ancient well of sorrows
dried up since the baroque years,
drenched Boehringer's ceiling down below,
his concert office closed at Pentecost.
A frog with immense white limbs
swims in the well.

And I'm walking with a gospel tune in mind
which Eddie sent over from the States.
Says life's a burden you can lay down.

Lay my-ah
burden down, go walking
go walking on the other side
of the Grands Boulevards;
neon silently barks at a pigeon
sends it up in flurries like a bat;
let it rest. See my-ah
dressed in his golf leathers
father there,
see my-ah
dressed in white hair
mother there,
see my-ah
dressed in her Pentecost
sister there,
see my-ah
dressed in stained feathers
baby son there.
No side on the other side.

See my father falling on the fairway
of his life. Light goes out,
but darkness won't descend
on featureless houses,
absence of mood,
golf course grass greying and serious,
the whack gone out of the game,
the blood gone out of the brain,
trees coming alive with night
but not releasing it.
No passion yet in this childhood of a thought.
Past time's a heron once
in the course pond:
straw leg dislocated in water clear to the bottom.

A lot is loaded down, settled for good.
But who's uneasy there no more?
Who's in trouble there no more?

See my mother lay her head,
flakes of soap on a transparent pillow
an empty memory fringed with lace
(the snow fell
on such a resting place),
an elderly woman lies down there
dressed in her last cardigan,
in her coma,
the watery pillow whirls with lights
and heart-beat oscillograph blips.
I will her soul to go if it wants to.
'Please go, wherever you are.'
It flurries upwards like a white bat.
Who took the soap flakes packet,

let the flakes float down?
I was thinking of Jean Cocteau.

Emotions stagger forwards
in these distracted counsels.
I turn my head:
a gate had fallen away in her face.
And I continue walking.

See my sister; when her mouth was
morphine-dry, God sent saliva,
so she could sing her valediction hymn.
My-ah burden down.
Her belief a fixed acquittal
in the *cause célèbre* of our lives,
and I had thoughts on another side
of my mind. Mine the pale legs
like a huge white frog, went swimming
off Grenada's Grande Anse jetty
in the Caribbean Sea. Journalists floated
round about; it was thunderous
night above truffled green waters
welling onto beach of palm shadows.
Dressed in stained leathers,
a bat flew low on the wave, up
sidelong through a lightning flash
and I was hot shit in that flash romance.
Back in Surrey there
saw my sister who revealed her face
brimming with mysterious fortune
the face of one who justly assumed
in her dying that she'd earned a heaven.
Something very God-like rose within her;
she was immeasurably superior to me then,

interrupted the purpled lightning.
Bade me goodbye from her armchair;
I withdrew with a curious grimace.

A lot is loaded down now, I say,
halfway become my nature.
And I go walking on the boulevards,
bail à céder, soldes,
a price is no price unless a sale price;
my elbows are itchier than in the old days,
each time in Paris I'm more settled in habit,
a journeyman of innocence:
behold this Faustian innocent,
shedding deaths of others
as he goes walking.

See my baby lay his head on a down pillow,
pigeons flurrying on the boulevards.
Lay my bird in down.
Well, Tom's long in his coffin, inside his altar,
in some cathedral I've made for him
lit by summer photographic flashes.
I scarcely dare cross those cracked flags.
Why do I see instead the electric figure
of a black abbot
flitting along the galleries like a bat
and into high doors?
You'll never know where he'll appear next
in these galleries of my unbelief.
I don't know where the abbot is now,
for I'm casting the deaths of others
like disjointed stones into the cathedral well.

I continue walking towards what remains.
The trail I have left is the trail left behind.

On this, my third time of living in Paris,
I know these memories as
the mere same endroits;
the voice that used to speak for me is still there,
but I'm learning to speak over it, catching
it up like an under-air
on the Grands Boulevards
pigeons high against empurpling clouds.

Forearms

A purple-haired woman
with a paper handkerchief for a face
runs down the rue des Messageries.
Between the perspective of buildings
tall crane idle against the lines of morning
and a doleful green lion with navy-blue eyes
tattering down to emerald wraiths
dissipates its body in smoke.
Among the stream of Lubavitchers
this Saturday from the synagogue
floats a half-transparent gesture
with a hand that turns in mid-air
and comes back boldly dark blue.
Feminine ginger forearms
poke from a national marine's white blouse,
black slacks and sailor boy hat,
red-head squatting on the pavement bollard
where rue Faubourg Poisonnières
widens for our supermarket;
could be any teenager's frail life,
enlisted to right our errors
of despair, aggression, superstition.
Cirrus on blue above.
Matt black fighter plane
dropped in the road by a child
sets its heel on the sparkling tarmac,
the silhouette of it skids about and becomes

curling tyre marks, or a relic of
a dangerous attitude, setting children's lives
at risk. Our corruption needs copious innocence
to work on: I remember green fields,
a cook crossing to the airmen's mess
at Innesbrook, cirrus on blue in that vignette.
They could enlist me then; they couldn't now.
That summer of '57, like a tornado
in my mind I tell you,
green imploding on black
like a green bomb splotch on the Suez Canal.
In this morning's sunshine,
a cook crossing now to the boulangerie
triggered that memory. Opening the *Trib*
two paces down from the Metro,
I see they opened fire on the President of Egypt
yesterday as his motorcade
drove to the Addis Ababa summit.
Nearly caused war with Sudan; young Egyptian
forearms writing out enlistment papers;
one day there's a youth's flayed arm but no youth,
green body tattering down in bomb smoke.

Chord

That point of light must be where chord begins;
it's a foam packaging fragment in the light breeze,
a zig-zagging snowflake down Cadet, whose heatwave
seems cold for a tiny season when really that's an
albino thunder fly or a single ping on my son's guitar
which without a chord would take its own life,
whether it knows the next ping's coming or not.

I hear, and the eye-mote accords; I mean
with this chord on Cadet, sundry arab gutturals
in the alimentation shops, Jewish whispers
on a Friday ready for Sabbath; I mean with chord of
tourist twangs in the hotel of black suitcases
flowing together in a heatwave certainly
cold within its season, growth marks and bruises
on melons and apples. Chord, some old crow
that rasps over muscadet in the crow bar,
pun donk donk, pun donk donk,
crowbar clunked by a hammer under the distant
screaming in the parc Montholon
where the SDF are the PDGs of sunny benches
overseeing children's work in the sandpit
and office women eating their salads for an hour.

Chord with misty yellow sound at its foot,
that light laid on gutter pools thatched
by garbage; still the sound rises
into mid-airs of complex strokes of people
topped far above by a Napoleonic hat
of thunder and blooded oranges rather smeary.

To the side, lunch time has a green handle
like a cup as if you could lift and drink
a colourous chord of flaming wires.

SDF = *Sans Domicile Fixe*, the Homeless
PDG = *Président Directeur-Général*, Chairman of the Board

A Little Night

A word to come lies in a little night
where ash is falling.
The word can't be this 'coffin',
lying in its candour, in its cinders.
Inside, the poet's too lazy in his death
to perform a truth singly. All's ambiguous.

Yet a coffin is blocked in boldly, I see,
under the washing down of night.
The cobalt blue cabinet's cut on a slant
with candelabra making mirrors
along its sides peopling it with mourners,
delegates from the governments of poetry
and from their industries, who appear
only as reflections of shoulders.
Hostility of moths round the candles.
Hostility of mouths still saying 'coffin'.

The coffin waits in this little night
for the whole day's train.

My own face, visible in the mirrors now,
is a bruise again floating in hints of crystal.
I don't *yearn* towards my shadow, bowing
to it, reaching out to find lost unity;
for if the shadow really touched my finger
untruth would constitute truth, whereas
as Buber knew, the process takes a *Thou*.

Our shadows lack performance;
they are a text created by the dusty mirror:
I do all the touching and my finger
returns with its ashen tip, as you
the reader, when you touch these unreal ashes
find your own finger-tip is clean.

In our candour to be truthful, we're very stern
and talk too much of loss, covering our truths
with ashes – like authoritarian fathers
who damn their sons with an over-strict word,
'You'll never amount to anything.'

The word I care about
(it's been lying inside the slant cabinet)
wakes and now performs itself:
The word becomes 'Celan', formerly Antschel:
the only poet I have to struggle against
because none wrote more beautifully post-war
of the perfection and terror of crystal.

The Weekend Curfew

After the weekend curfew Celan
found the house
shuttered
the parents in captivity
himself condemned
to being enemy of himself.
His *Todesfuge*
began. Later that lyric
was, for many years,
an urn carried in German
ceremonies of forgetfulness
disguised as memory.
And so
Celan smashed it
with his intellect's hammer.

For Nazi cruelty in its pure light
had filled that lyric,
a vessel of the Sephiroth,
and when the hammer broke it
musical fragments
became shards,
part of the song went hiding
silent in stones,
dark rising past the
secretly-glowing
stones on ashheaps,
words that
each whip

stroke cracked open
in savage light.

And we, we'd emulate this,
letting our lyrics croak
the throat
into broken music
as if mere self-unease
were our righteousness
smashing the lyric vessel
in darkness
so to be as smart as he was
oh to be as smart as he was
our words nowhere near bursting
with such a lesser weight of light,
as we flip through
the fragments
of our cheque book stubs.

'Evening descending mauve'

For Gisèle Celan-Lestrange

Evening descending mauve
on the rue Montorgeuil,
presenting on the palm of the sky
a navy-blue bruise,
an old Jewish wound,
not a nail-hole.

I go calling on Gisèle again
in my mind,
to thank her for a New Year etching
of rocks that were almost rain.

Her face with its knowledge of suicide,
her low voice and cancer-death
easily haunt me now.
I had a skyscape in her pastels,
half-owned by a friend,
six months a time on our walls;
its troublesome clouds
were also rocks bruising land.
Now her life seems a diptych to me
of joy and fire one side,
the other, later side mauve
as prison camp snow.
Her husband Celan's
early poem to his parents
shot by the Germans
takes on new meaning:
'You didn't die the mauve death'
(of cyanide gas).

Shocked by unsuspected absence,
I return on the straight road
past Heine's lodgings
to my fishcarter's faubourg.
Gisèle calls me from the outerworld
– once the call was real,
but this is the haunting –
and I half-hear her lovely reply
to a chance remark at dinner
on the Montorgeuil. I'd told her:

'A poet's suicide may
for a moment cut the path
of the past to the future'
(because there is no bridge
across its dreadful river banks,
though the path one day reforms
after so great a life
as an Iris bridge, yet of stone too).
For a tactless moment the room
became her husband's grave,
in the far wild water a file opening.

While I live Gisèle calls me
frequently to say,
'*Ça m'a profondement touchée,*'
taking part-ownership in the remark,
so that I become moved
by the iridescent bridges of Celan
and of Celan-Lestrange.

Trink

The flat's stifling, I leave two paintings on my desk,
go out on Faubourg Poisonnières, look towards the Seine,
down the straight road to Montorgeuil again;
the after-Sabbath sun lays its baked cream light
on tenements whose shutters sew it on flat
with shadow stitches narrowing in long lines.

A dazzle of messy rays, makes a lion-clawed curtain
with brush-strokes of orange straw,
seared skin, grains of dried blood, it hangs
in my way, Lion of Judah or Christian apocalypse,
whose angel trumpets heralded this fiery air.
Far behind the hot curtain where I can't get at it,
beyond these faubourg reaches, at the river
where bridges end the lyric, there's still snow
snow lying like a private drift of death
filling the bridge arches, or at least I feel so.
But the curtain's radiant with creation's colours;
they make a moment in the sun when all religions
lie open and I may envision them without blasphemy
although their doors are closed to me and, said
Celan, the Lion of Judah bars the royal road.
That's the counter movement: beyond the heat's caesura,
the absent prosody consorts with the here-to-now.
Black yarmulkes pass by me to Beth Din shops.

I don't walk down to Montorgeuil this time,
but stay in sunshine on the lion side, here
where Heine, whose paralysis was first of fingers,
then of lips, wrote his poems in letters
one inch high; a morphine wound at the neck, he,
unable to kiss, pushing his eyelid up to see his guests,
making out he had *le droit de moribondage*,
the right of being mortally ill, though he could lie
only on one side in the Faubourg Poisonnières,
weep out of one eye only, and joked
that he could claim only half a woman's heart.
And he had half Mathilde's. This death,
this mattress-grave, Heine gave us so
sardonically. But I admire as much an unknown
grandmother, an eighty-year-old in Brightlingsea, who,

with the same spinal atrophy, died as fine a death
before my eyes. Or my stout-heart, Ted Berrigan,
fighting demons to the end of his own red shift,
until they departed, the world's furious
song flowing through his costume, thus to me.

I find the lion-curtain back at home all along,
in a diptych by Joan Mitchell, the one side
called 'Cobalt', with mauve snow and a blue
coffin: the other *Pour ses malinois*,
savagely blazing, tawny orange, racy yellows
almost curtaining a similar coffin, similar snow.
You see I'm not lying, not even figuratively.

Now I set the paintings up by my computer.
They're like a Christian reredos to a Seder
and curiously please me. So I place
three glasses of wine before the screen
and make a poetic communion. The two
standing before 'Cobalt' symbolize Celan's
'*Ich trink Wein aus zwei Gläsern*',
as if he'd been caught between Aleph and Youd,
with a lion-blocked caesura between them, a silence,
Aleph of the divine commandments, and Youd,
God's first letter blasphemed by the Germans
into Yid martyrs in the snow. The other glass,
'*Pour ses malinois*', I dedicate to Heine;
remember, oh remember how he lay
crippled on his eight-year grave and in his wine
saw his young self drinking in a tavern
mocking the pain in his spine; yet he never
ceased his songs of 'joy and fire' and wrote
of Richard Lion-Heart riding in English forests,
free from Austrian prisons.

In admiration of Heine I drink his glass,
I drink it for his cheerful wife, Mathilde,
for Gisèle, for Ted, for a certain Mrs Foster;
I look down a red throat at the liquid's
peristaltic whirling in the bowl and so I swallow.

In even deeper homage to Celan's integrity
I pour his two glasses away.

Someone's God's tongue
licks all three glasses clean.

Crystal Eagle 1

In Memoriam Paul Celan

A crystal eagle tied by the neck
with soft silk braid, like a unicorn
restrained by a virgin, sneers
and draws in snow crystals of its breath
when I move my head to make lights
travel along its beak. There's future
silence of the non-forthcoming in the rue
de Paradis shop window – rue
de Paradis once the près-des-filles-Dieu.
Villeroy & Boch have laid five glass hearts
around the eagle plinth, gold-amber,
lemon, red, blue, purple, whose bruises
slide within the under-wings. Myself
a stranger at home in this widowed

Jewish crystal quarter, I muse
on a suicide that I can't in all decency
address as *tu*. But if I could,
the silken braid would fall, the eagle
rising, draw a chariot through the sky
towards mauve snow around a throne,
centre of all that's celestial in Celan.

Crystal Eagle 2

Incipit. God said 'eagle' and an eagle flew
out of the pages of the Kabbalah. The gullible
poets said, 'Nowadays, the world approaches us
already pregnant with foetal language.' Are they
mentally ill to think language so divine?
Did God say 'crystal eagle' and this one
in a rue de Paradis window didn't fly?
It has that neck cord for stability or anti-theft,
that surround of glass hearts reflected in the crystal,
the eagle's shoulder in a dark coat snuggling into
great masses of snow. Gold-amber's for its eye,
lemon's for the distant sun, purple's for royal
emotions aroused in the lurid eagle on its crag
when thunder strikes beneath its plumes.
Red's for blood springing from the mouth
of an eagle stoned by a snowball in a courtyard
when it swallows down a Kabbalistic silence.
Blue's for the bird's flight far from the rue Bleue
that runs north round here from Paradis.

Then the poem-words, 'rue Bleue', do make the eagle
fly a little? No: perch on a wrist. I'll tell you.
I've been away to Epping Forest, England,
whose real trees taking over this mind-landscape
had blue between their tops as clouds began to end
a heatwave. Suddenly, a wattle
fence became transparent as the sun
brightened a clearing behind. A falconer
in heavy boots stumped into view, a barn owl
on one shoulder, a golden eagle on the wrist.

The owl made him lean to that side, the eagle
young but heavy on his glove; he walked
with crooked steps through the newly-green trees.
Don't you think you've just read that in a poem?
Returned to Paris, I make a blue filter slide
over my memory of the falconer's steps,
his black trousers crossing like chromosomes.

Rue Bleue itself wasn't blue anyway, being so
near Paradis they called it 'rue d'Enfer'.
Those who lived there changed its name to Bleue.
A few blue glints – window reflections, a car passing,
a woman's shorts – plunge my mind
on the rue Bleue deep into a vivid valley I know
in an abstract painting. I'll call it the Kabbalistic
'Abyss of Good'. At that, ultramarine
mud gets swabbed with cobalt in a wink.
Paradise erupts there in yellow anemones
under the bungling Prussian blue foliage;
the watery silhouette of a crimson forest
is like a tattered horizon, blood washed down
the easel-slope. Broken-legged chromosomes
in the foreground. How can this painting
and my life, quite other than it, match so well?
But the patterns of seeing form in memory patterns
held in patterns of language. Did I say
'Easel'? *Incipit*. The crystal eagle
from rue Paradis flies over this painted landscape.
The painter called it not the Blue, not the Crystal, not
the Epping, not the Good, but the Grand Valley.

From rue d'Enfer to rue Bleue Again

Heaven and hell obviously split-mind stuff, like
laying the same on the same, blue doubled on blue,
yellow gulping up in laughter to the skies, or
black and fire on black and fire, with reddened anger
burning at the bottom. Heaven is happiness
multiplied by the infinity of the instant, blanked
off from Hell's anger-fear trapped in its own
blind instant.

In this intense mood, I try to see inside
the cat-box that Schrödinger left in a car
outside Heine's house where I cross the road
as usual and go for croissants on the rue Bleue.
No sound comes from the breathing holes.
It's not the animal that's dead but thought itself
trying to make the opposites of life or death
interpenetrate.

Here's a shop on the rue Bleue that sells brass
and only brass, long rails of it, door handles
and a measuring counter in the empty spaces.
That's same on same, but only like habit, like
having your coffee every morning with the croissant.
To see brass and then again brass, forever
staring at the same brass plate in the shop window,
takes you within brass.

And seeing piano wood and again piano wood takes
you within all tunes pianos might play. I turn
into the boulangerie where the croissants
bite each other in rows. That's just crabby habit,
repetition of detail. The smoothness of brass
is easier to see, same on its same, than rough pastry.
And a manic emotion takes you inside itself and then
inside itself again.

Light in Back

The streets were blasted by road works.
Tar mazes, black cravid, flame skirts,
stimplumzitt of tar damper, sear ooze
(the two-word stage of acquiring poetry
from some complete moment), wild it with fa,
grossly about ambition, excess lipid,
try vivid, or limpid, try vivid, yes vivid,
make lold. In their moment those words
anticipated sorrows like people who'll be
lost to us in our future, a vanished race
of tall skirts dressed in old altar cloths.
I can't hand on poetry while it's in
this state, widowed by words I married.

Sun buzz had made the windows
grey with dust on the rue de Trevise;
that street noise, alive, began fading
as twilight fell. *Hear, O Israel* was shut.
An old man's torch wobbled its beam
around the bookshop's far back room;
torch beams fringed his beard of truth;
in the window, minorahs and bechers.
My eyes travelled on from ritual objects
through the word to his light. Make lold.
We can't remain windowed by words,
must intuit origin. And so this past
immediately becomes news to hand on.

My poorly-made road's good only
for a word-created world, a glued-together

alphabet sphere spinning in bluish plastic.
I'm lonely of it. But I thought-created
a lot of worlds in the space before this one,
as I stood at the rue de Trevise window,
my words about to begin in already faded
yellow air above the road machines –
a possible million of worlds in their lumps,
or luminous imaginings, red shifting,
uninformed by languages, but *en voyage*
to the harlequin light of beginning
terrifying or utterly quiet.

Walnut and Lily

And even if rose and nightingale
were fabricating what they feel, it would have
some benefit, as so often befalls.
                              – Heine, *Neue Gedicht*

White undervest nestling on black trousers
creeping round the bookcase in dawn light
seen before getting up to make coffee,
sad water lily under a love-pained moon.

That was said while tucking in a shirt,
a Heine piece of beautiful shit, said in thuds
for I keeled over dying on the floored mattress.
Nearly as bad as, 'the void, the silence, the space
inside the word', a crock, this time, of shit
at a Celan conference – might as well crack open

walnuts with their diploid kernels, or set walnut
words bobbing about on a lake in a lyric,
ripples with narrow paddles of moonlight in hollows.

A breakfast sparrow chirps. Choosing a jacket,
I seem to have only two choices these days,
not the old romantic tweed but middle-age black
and Celanian gloom: I worry about Britain fallen
to gnawing its kernel. Today, a middle-class tie,
a nutty shade, honouring those architectonic
word knots of Celan, little tie nuts. *Die nachtigall!*

No Heine nightingales in Paris. Still half-dreaming,
I'm by a lake rescuing walnuts from the flood
(just a few last cornflakes in the bowl) and am
obscurely angry. Suppose our words cracked open
to another kind of light, not 'white void';
crack open Celan's hard-won 'thought scarab';
crack open 'animal-bloodblooming';
crack open 'net-nerved skyleaf'.

See the walnuts in my dream-lake
rippling along like turds in creaming dawn,
or imagine a black scarab floating there,
make its carapace bloom with a lily.
Lift a precious walnut from out the waters
thumb its wet shell open. Don't kid me, you don't
find silence inside but red heat, a tiny furnace.

Instead of that well-gnawed British despair
instead of return to a middle-class Parnassus,
these words are angry, in a flood of lyric feeling:
I return the black jacket, put on the frayed tweed,
replace the tie, still knotted, in the cupboard.

Twilight Flowers

By Heine's house a flower shop reopens;
the school *rentrée* ends a classic summer
and black grape-skins lie in the crimson throats
of dahlias watered by many lives of people
I once caused to cry and now remember
this September birthday harvesting. Also,
others worry me today: you insulted my angel;
you won't relinquish literary snobbery;
you reduce my meanings to linguistic paradox.
So I become a hermit, though constantly with friends,
a Scotsman assimilated into England and America.
Resisting the call of cold singers,
I'm back in France with others' grapes for wine.
Soon, a new vintage. Yes but I planted a rotten stock
down by an English estuary one springtime,
a sour wine after twenty fruitful years;
instead, pass me Heine, with his tart wine-uh;
I'm thinking of his Götterdammerung,
where the greenest of Mays became a horror film
of human evils and titans toppled the gods.

Who are my gods? My own wronged ones
and certain others: Celan, Gisèle . . . not Heidegger,
for he's an enemy who combed the Lorelei's
golden hair while muttering how profound is
care in the groundwork of being. But it's Heine,
the assimilator, who rises from these dahlia flames.
Smoke at twilight clouds his body with legends,
his shoulder a blue cliff and poking out
from the giant's sleeve his tiny writing hand,

half paralysed by spinal illness,
keeps pecking hungrily like a black pullet.
When his May's earth became transparent
in the twilight of the gods and the tombs glowed
with putrescent limbs, and when the titans,
fawned on by their dwarves, erected ladders out of hell,
and charged the elaborate thrones of heaven,
that hand pecked away until he set his old love
among the angels to be raped by demons.
In the twilight of our values I suppose those
we've loved unhappily will be sitting in the heavens
as usual, stupefied, like a television audience
watching war scenes, when dwarves in our imagination's
pay yank them off their crimsoned thrones
and commit unspeakable acts among the flames.

A woman moans in her harmonica a last time:
she's neurotic and clatters down the stairs to us
complaining of a light tapping in her room.
Retreating sweetly, her face ruined by neglect,
she says it's not our computers but a stranger signal,
and to me it sounds like the death-watch beetle.
As I restart, pitch glistens on my typing fingers,
my fingernails black chestnuts; an autumnal
infection blacker than bruising darkens
the whole hand whitened with kaolin dribbles.
Fingers type from out my shirt, my own blue cliff,
while ant-like letters appear on dahlia petals,
and trail into the crimson throats of flames.
At last all rests; an electric bulb, switched on,
highlights my wine. It's to Heine's violated angel
that I offer my new vintage in the twilight
of all gods, not the twilight of all values.

Denise Riley

Laibach Lyrik: Slovenia, 1991

The milky sheen of birch trees
stepping forward. Breathless
the deeper woods.

Goldfinches rattle down
through branches, leap
and sparkle off to dusk.

Below a mass of cloud this evening
a faintly orange light
slides on your lifting smile.

Afternoon's blue winds dropped
now wreaths of raspberry smoke
pat the steady sky.

Cream fields chat quietly
careless of distant provinces
and the guns of rebels.

Whooping cranes rise where
herdsmen, clattering, wheel about
the plains in scarlet.

Cut the slavonics now. Cut the slavonics.
Slovenian and all other civil planes are off.
The federal airforce has the skies sewn up.
The snows come early, Austrian lorries slide
across the mountain pass in slow veers sidelong
skate gingerly to fates, grand destinies dreamily chosen.
Entering Yugoslavia we aren't there, we are straight into Slovenia instead
late at night, frozen, instantly crazy with obsessive and terrible tendernes

again; unable to find my passport. Napoléon, sauveur of Illyria! whose
monument in Ljubljana spells out in gleams of gold calligraphy, Our
   Liberty.
Here videos of the summer bombings, entitled the Triumph of Slovenia,
   or
How a Nation Awoke, are wrapped in paper jackets showing fighter
   planes
with yellow extension-lead cables, mortar smoke, on stalls with t-shirts,
logos of the state. The country restaurant pipes a first-time go
at national music to its dining rooms, unclear what that should sound
   like;
oompah Bavarian results, mortifying to the city friends, who disconnect
its speakers, drawing down a ruddy glare of sausages, peasant style.
Rain darkens the fish-scale roofs of the provincial capital. In London
temporary exiles meet, some in despair about their forced new names
others worn down with dislocation, with explaining histories
to well-meant local ignorant evenhandedness. A girl calls out 'This time
last year, we none of us knew or cared. The cars streamed down all
   summer
to the Dalmatian coast from Serbia, and so what. Did I grow up for
   this
to take new designations, learn to hate my neighbours, just because of
   where
I came from, which I never used to know? The last war stopped
before my mother's birth. Who says I must be "Bosnian" now.
I grew up Yugoslavian. Just stop this craziness, these killings.' Another,
older, says 'It is a lie that walls are coming down in Europe. We see
   them rise
and we are penned inside. The deaths of twenty thousand make me this
that I don't want to be. But that blood lost means I must take that
   name –
though not that politics – must be, no not a nationalist, yet ambiguously
   Croatian

must be it through the dictates of those deaths alone. We should, all
    should —
look forward, must rebuild . . .' She stops. I'm seeing present history
glance round it for support, I'm hearing it at work to stammer its
    imperfect story
go on too long, be conscientious, grab at straws, then reach its edge of
    tears.

I'm not these, never could be, am by accident of place of birth protected,
    yet exactly as
this nation-sheltered onlooker, must try to think. The room splits into
    clumps and fights.
Outsiders now move off, get back to native non-community, and across
    real distances
made semi-manageable through irony; so that I'll say I've stood here as
    a dark stand of trees,
still, sealed black, outwardly silent but vibrantly loud inside with others'
    gossip about itself
like 'the unconscious'; and I'll leave as I might leave a party whose
    guests were venomous
yet inconsolable, deliberately straightening my shoulders and saying
    aloud, although
to nobody in particular, It's good to get some air.
The usual spectator's cocky journey home through stupidness.
This evening's tongues go scrapping on till dawn:

The settling scar agrees to voice
what seems to speak its earliest cut.
A rage to be some wholeness gropes

past damage that it half recalls —
where it was, I will found my name.
A hesitant gap now stretches its

raw mouth: I will become this sex
and Istrian. And still at night
hair dazzles in white lights

from flares. A greenish patina
may roughen these spent shells
for future curious songs. Now people

and their resonant cities are obliterated.
What is it that shapes us, whether
we will or no, that through these

opened and reopened mouths that form
the hollow of a speaking wound, we
come to say, yes, now we are Illyrian.

A Shortened Set

All the connectives of right recall
have grown askew. I know
a child could have lived, that
my body was cut. This cut
my memory half-sealed but glued
the edges together awry.
The skin is distorted, the scar-tissue
does damage, the accounts are wrong.
And this is called 'the healing process'.
Now nothing's aligned properly.
It's a barbarous zone.
The bad sutures
thicken with loss and hope –
brilliant, deliberate
shaking patients in an anteroom
refusing the years, ferocious to be called
so I'll snip through the puckered skin
to where they tug for re-aligning. Now
steady me against inaccuracy, a lyric urge
to showing-off. The easy knife
is in my hand again. Protect me.

Small is the history, and dark.
Its purplish valleys are unfurled
as the militant trees clash over it together.
I'd long in its steep descent to slip
past fuss and toughness to escape
both well-oiled grief and an escaper's
cheery whistling. Tedious. This

representing yourself, desperate to get it right,
as if you could, is that the aim of the writing?
'I haven't got off lightly, but I got off' – that won't
deflect your eyes that track you through the dark.
There is the traveller, there the decline
and his sex that the journey strips from him. A
perfectly democratic loneliness sets out
down the mined routes of speaking to its life.
So massively, gently, should it go
that it might overtake
even the neatest Professor of Speed.

The last sun on dark red brick burns violet-black where
I wait to get back something in the narrows of the city
under its great sides, whose brick or painted walls
glow into the paler light above them, a hugely quiet halo
formed from the internal heat of rooftops. These seep
their day off to the sky cupped very coolly distant
over this tight rim. My heart takes grateful note
to be in life, the late heat shaped in bricks of air
stuck out, hot ghosts to catch my hand on.
The slap of recognition that you know.
Your feelings, I mean mine, are common to us all:
that puts you square between relief and boredom
under the standoffish sky.
In this I'm not unique, I'm just
the only one who thinks I'm not, maybe.

How can black paint be warm? It is. As ochre
stains slip into flooding milk, to the soft black
that glows and clots in sooty swathes.
Its edges rust, it bleeds lamp-black
slow pools, as planes of dragged cream

shoot over it to whiteness, layered.
Or the cream paint, leaden, wrinkles: birch bark
in slabs, streaked over a peeling blue. A twist
of thought is pinned there. A sexual black. And I
can't find my way home. Yet wandering there I may.
By these snow graphics. Ice glazed
to a grey sheen, hard across dark grass spikes.

Is that what's going on – the slow
replacement of a set of violent feelings
by neutral ones. The hell if so.
There has been damage, which must stop at me.
I think that's finished. Then the underside
of a brushed wing unsettles things.
I'd cup that powdery trace in mind
like a big moth in a matchbox, whirring.

Are you alright I ask out there
straining into the dusk to hear.
I think its listening particles of air
at you like shot.
You're being called across your work
or – No I don't want that thought.
Nor want to get this noise to the point
it interests me. It's to you. Stop.

But

Am I alright you don't ask me.
Oh probably, and in the heart
of this light on hills it is for me
alone to speak. No triumph.
This milky light's a fact and the broad air

and the strip of primrose water, a long way down.
That red dot is my car, let's go

Or let I go.

– That black dot was myself.
I strike you as complete:
a late unpacking in life
in hope of a human view.
After these nights of rain on
the mountain the water's running
so hard it's marbled white
the streams like heavy snow.
Deletions are sifting down
onto the study floor – Cut
more cut more, mutter my
hearing creatures, snouts
rooting upward for light.
They push to nudge my
failures aside and go but
what would become of me in
the quiet once they were out.
Will you be good towards
these animals of unease
I can just about call them home:

Coffee goes coppery on my tongue today
as 'Let's Dance' is hammered out again on the radio.
It was my party and I wept not wanting to.
'Mother of children, don't go into the house in the dark.'
Letters crash onto the hall floor with their weight of
    intelligence and junk.
I get up with hope for them, until word may finally arrive.

It is called feeling but is its real name thought?
Moons in their spheres are not so bland as these.
A round O says I feel and all agree.
Walking by many on London streets
in a despair which carries me
I look from face to face like a dog going
in the social democracy of loneliness.
May move instead through a shimmer
around me of racial beauty crying like something expensive
    which
breaks into eyes sparkling all over skin.

It's that simple
in another town.
No, it doesn't know me
nor this train I'm on.

The ex-poet's beside herself:
'Here in the clouded
red, the grey, the burnt
oak forest, the rails shake'

Safely I'll love it by letter
yet skip the 'better
that way' to cancel
the doubter's rhyme, trembling.

Aha we are frozen
stiff as young hyacinths –
outrageous blue
decides to leave green.

I'd drive anywhere with anyone, just
to have that held sense of looking out

from a container, amiably, stolidly, while
I'm portered by. Along the ring-road
murmurous orange lights on stilts with
necks stuck out like herons on the grey
slipway, angled above the cars repeating
themselves fast and fast as if they were one.
When I'm unloaded and stood in dread
at home encircled by my life, whose
edges do show – then I so want it to run
and run again, the solitary travelling perception.
Road movie: Protectedness, or, Gets through time.

An ice blue calm, violently sustained
has got to know a thing about this nation
and our being in it.
How do I act, then, properly
without a sticky modesty
in the crammed-fullness of the place
too dense for story threads to pierce?
I'm quiet. I'm at the end of all opinion.
Should I not know where clearness lies.
Time has run short and I need company
to crack my separate stupidity. I'd thought
to ask around, what's lyric poetry?
Its bee noise starts before I can:
You do that; love me; die alone.

Don't quote the 'we'
of pairs nor worse, of sentient
humanity, thanks.

That's attitudinizing, in those
three lines. That's what I do.

Help me out of it, you
you sentient humanity.

I was signed up for a course
on earth by two others who left me and
left me impossibly slow at Life Skills

at admitting unlikeness or grasping the
dodgem collision whose shock isn't
truth but like the spine says is no

deception. I hate the word
collusion used of love but in the end
I wasn't anyone else ever –

that I sweated blood to force
lucidity to come as if headlocked
by history, to explain I really was –

all that was powered by desperation –
the thought of it makes me mortified.
Then after years, so-whattish:

The loves are returned to
themselves, leaving
an out post-sexual.

Unanxious, today.
A feeling of rain
and dark happiness.

Rain slops into dust
caught underfoot
in short grit runnels.

Faint news from the wharf
peppered on skin in

fresh patters of rain.

The evening lightens.
A friend's shout
blown inaudibly.

Sit. See, from the riverside
winds buzz new towers
of puzzling wealth.

Curved to this view
the gleam of a moment's
social rest.

Hair lit to a cloud
the sunlight lowering
first hesitant then strong.

In a rush
the glide of the heart
out on a flood of ease.

Wherever You Are, Be Somewhere Else

A body shot through, perforated, a tin sheet
beaten out then peppered with thin holes,
silvery, leaf-curled at their edges; light flies

right through this tracery, voices leap, slip sidelong, all faces split to angled facets: whichever
piece is glimpsed, that bit is what I am, held

in a look until dropped like an egg on the floor
let slop, crashed to slide and run, yolk yellow
for the live, the dead who worked through me.

Out of their lined shell the young snakes broke
past skin fronds stretched over sunless colour or
lit at a slant, or saturated grey – a fringe flapping

round nothing, frayed on a gape of glass, perspex
seen through, seen past, no name, just scrappy
filaments lifting and lifting over in the wind.

Draw the night right up over my eyes so that I
don't see and then I'm gone; push the soft hem
of the night into my mouth so that I stay quiet

when an old breeze buffets my face to muffle
me in terror of being left, or is that a far worse
terror of not being left. No. Inching flat out

over a glacier overhanging blackness I see no
edge but will tip where its glassy cold may stop
short and hard ice crash to dark air. What do

the worms sing, rearing up at the threshold?
Floating a plain globe goes, the sky closes.
But I did see by it a soul trot on ahead of me.

I can try on these gothic riffs, they do make
a black twitchy cloak to both ham up and so
perversely dignify my usual fear of ends.

To stare at nothing, just to get it right, get
nothing right, with some faint idea of this
as a proper way to spend a life. No, what

I really mean to say instead is, come back
won't you, just all of you come back, and give
me one more go at doing it all again but doing it

far better this time round – the work, the love stuff –
so I go to the wordprocessor longing for line cables
to loop out of the machine straight to my head

and back, as I do want to be only transmission –
in sleep alone I get articulate to mouth the part of
anyone and reel off others' characters until the focus

of a day through one-eyed self sets in again: go into it.
I must. *The flower breaks open to its bell of sound
that rings out through the woods.* I eat my knuckles

hearing that. I've only earned a modern, what, a flatness.
Or no, I can earn nothing, but maybe
some right to stop now and to say to you, Tell me.

– That plea for mutuality's not true. It's more ordinary that
flying light should flap me away into a stream of specks
a million surfaces without a tongue and I never have wanted

'a voice' anyway, nor got it. Alright. *No silver coin has been*
nailed to your house's forehead you dog-skin among the fox fur
where did you get that rosewater to make your skin so white?

I did get that rosewater before I came to the light grass
shakes in a wind running wild over tassels of barley
the sails were of the light green silk sewn of both gold

and white money take down take down the sails of silk set up
the sails of skin and something dark and blurred upon the
    ground
where something else patrols it, cool, nervous, calling out

Stop now. Hold it there. Balance. Be beautiful. Try.
– And I can't do this. I can't talk like any of this.
You hear me not do it.

Lure, 1963

Navy near-black cut in with lemon, fruity bright lime green.
I roam around around around around acidic yellows, globe
oranges burning, slashed cream, huge scarlet flowing
anemones, barbaric pink singing, radiant weeping When
will I be loved? Flood, drag to papery long brushes
of deep violet, that's where it is, indigo, oh no, it's in
his kiss. Lime brilliance. Obsessive song. Ink tongues.
Black cascades trail and spatter darkly orange pools
toward washed lakes, whose welling rose and milk
beribboned pillars melt and sag, I'm just a crimson
kid that you won't date. Pear glow boys. Clean red.

Fluent grey green, pine, broad stinging blue rough
strips to make this floating space a burning place of
whitest shores, a wave out on the ocean could never
move that way, flower, swell, don't ever make her blue.
Oh yes I'm the great pretender. Red lays a stripe of darkest
green on dark. My need is such I pretend too much, I'm
wearing. And you're not listening to a word I say.

A Misremembered Lyric

A misremembered lyric: a soft catch of its song
whirrs in my throat. 'Something's gotta hold of my heart
tearing my' soul and my conscience apart, long after
presence is clean gone and leaves unfurnished no
shadow. Rain lyrics. Yes, then the rain lyrics fall.
I don't want absence to be this beautiful.
It shouldn't be; in fact I know it wasn't, while
'everything that consoles is false' is off the point –
you get no consolation anyway until your memory's
dead: or something never had gotten hold of
your heart in the first place, and that's the fear thought.
Do shrimps make good mothers? Yes they do.
There is no beauty out of loss; can't do it –
and once the falling rain starts on the upturned
leaves, and I listen to the rhythm of unhappy pleasure
what I hear is bossy death telling me which way to
go, what I see is a pool with an eye in it. Still let
me know. Looking for a brand-new start. Oh and never
notice yourself ever. As in life you don't.

Poem Beginning with a Line from Proverbs

As iron sharpens iron
I sharpen the face of my friend
so hard he sings out
in high delicate notes.

A struggle for mastery to most speak
powerful beauty would run any
attention or kindness clean out
of town in angry rags.

Ringed by darkness the heart pulsates.
And power comes in like lightning.
A lion in the room, fair and flowing
twists with unsparing eyes.

Whitely the glance runs
to it and away. But let it
talk its golden talk if we
don't understand it.

Grabbed by remote music
I'm frightening myself. Speak
steadily as is needed to
stare down beauty. That calms it.

Lyric

Stammering it fights to get
held and to never get held
as whatever motors it swells
to hammer itself out on me

then it can call out high
and rounded as a night
bird's cry falling clean
down out of a black tree.

I take on its rage at the cost
of sleep. If I love it I sink
attracting its hatred. If I
don't love it I steal its music.

Take up a pleat in this awful
process and then fold me flat
inside it so that I don't see
where I was already knotted in.

It is my burden and subject
to listen for sweetness in hope
to hold it in weeping ears though
each hurt each never so much.

Song

Some very dark blue hyacinths on the table
A confession or two before dusk
flings open the fridge with loud relief
Listen honey I

A warm disturbing wind cruises the high road

where in curtained rooms children
are being beaten then so am I again but no one's
asking for it, I'm asking for something different now

Rayon

The day is nervous buff – the shakiness, is it inside the day
   or me?
Perhaps the passions that we feel don't quite belong to
   anyone
but hang outside us in the light like hoverflies, aping wasps
   and swivelling
and lashing up one storm of stripes. In tiny cones of air.
Yet you enact that feeling, as you usually *bzzzzzzzzz* get to
   do it, while I,
I do this. If it takes me all night and day. Oh Carol.

Well All Right

Above, a flurry of swans, brothers, great wings airy
around my bowed head in rushing darkness, neatly
these bone fingers plaited their green cloaks each night
to unfeather them so now they stand upright before me
freed and gaily they leap to their caparisoned horses as
in my breathing cell I smooth down my own cloak of
nettles – but Grimm sweetie mediaeval griseldas, right
out on the night plains are no tiny lights of huddlement
but only the impersonal stars in blackness and the long
long winds. What you see is what you see: it's never
what you won't. Well all right things happened it would
be pleasanter not to recall, as a deeply embarrassed dog
looks studiedly at a sofa for just anything to do instead,
so determine to assume events silently with no fuss –
who doesn't try to – yes that is a dart in my neck and
doesn't it look a bit biedermeier – so take up that thud
of attack dropped out of a righteously wide-open beak
sailing slowly across its own high sky which you'd not
registered as contempt straight out to kill – far rather
than know that, wear it as an owned cloak's blazing
fabric stuck in the fine flesh of your shoulders like any
natural skin burning; so cloaked, no one sees through
to you wrapped in darkness, only a darkness pressed to
outward navy twill – no queen of the night's gorgeous
winking suit, just suave cheap unexceptional off any
rack – want to slip out of it? but flesh has soaked to join
its fiery choric costume. Break out in flames. Leap to
the crests of orange birds flickering along the long line
of shoulders, hiss, warble in gaping whistles hoarse lyre

chants of plumed and swollen throats whose glowing trills
waver and zigzag the swayed neck heavy under the flare
song of any body glittering with hard memory. Let fall
this garment with its noisy wings. Slide from me now –
and let's just run something red and stinging rapidly down
the page, shall we, let's try an echt gloss speed placing
let's stand back in triumph dripping brushes, shall we
see what can be made out of this lot my lot, its lovely
trailed gash wet as a frock in a pool, what it's for is for
defence, it will keep your beautiful soul glazed as a
skein of floating hill mist and as quietly as slightly
and as palely lit – at risk of frank indifference it may
make beauty to sleep and, or, to sleep with. Who sang
'you don't have to die before you live' – well who.

The Castalian Spring

I

A gush of water, welling from some cave, which slopped
down to a stone trough squatting stout and chalky as a
morning sky: I plumped myself on lizard-ridden stone to stare
into its old truth square that struck me as perhaps another lie
so serious did it look while it promised me, oh, everything.
That honest look of water nursed in stone excited me. Under
the generous trees, tall splotchy planes and brittle ilex, their
dark flopped down, sun-glare and dust spun through it.

2

I sipped that cold and leafy water tentatively, lost lipstick
dabbing my mouth, gulped down a little slippery grit I hoped
was not ferny mosquito larvae; then sat on, guidebook-learned
to get gorgeous and pneumatic in the throat, my bulk deflating
slowly until the sunset, when the last coach parties slid away.
The heat of the day peeled off, the light got blurred and hummed,
pounding dusk struck up then a strong swelling rose in my throat
thick with significant utterance. So, shivery in my cool and newly
warty skin, I raised this novel voice to honk and boom.

3

I was small enough now, and stoical, to squat on the slabs of rock
edging the trough, splashed with the spring that welled steadily into it
shaking its stone-cupped water. I wear yet a precious jewel in my head
I mused, this line of old rhetoric floating back through me, as quite
unsurprised I settled to study the night, flexing my long damp thighs
now as studded and ridged as the best dill pickles in Whitechapel.

nto the cooling air I gave tongue, my ears blurred with the lyre
of my larynx, its vibrato reverberant into the struck-dumb dusk.

4

What should I sing out on this gratuitous new instrument?
Not much liking minimalism, I tried out some Messiaen,
found I was as natural as a bassoon, indeed the ondes martenot
simply oozed out of me. Or should lyric well up less, be bonier?
So I fluted like HD's muse in spiky girlish hellenics, slimmed
my voice down to twig-size, so shooting out stiffly it quivered
in firework bursts of sharp flowers. Or had I a responsibility to
speak to society: though how could it hear me? It lay in its hotels.

5

I spun out some long lines, let them loop in sound ribbons
lassoed the high branches where they dangled and trailed
landing like leathery bats in vacancy – alighted, they pleated,
composed themselves flawlessly, as lifeless as gloves.
The silence that hung on these sounds made me sheepish.
I fished for my German, broke out into lieder, rhymed
Sieg with *Krieg*, so explaining our century; I was hooked
on my theory of militarism as stemming from lyricism.

6

I'd crouched close by a cemetery; at twilight its keeper
lit oil lamps in shrines on the pale marble graves, each
brandishing silver-framed photographs; fresh flowers
for the well-furnished dead shone out amiably, while
the scops owl in residence served up its decorous gulps.
Lights burned on steadfastly in this town of the dead,
each soul in for a long night, their curtains undrawn.
My monotone croaking rang crude in such company.

7

Black plane trees bent over me, crouched in the night breeze.
For hours I called out on a sonorous roll, growing somewhat self-
conscious I'd nothing to do but to sound: yet sound was so stirring
and beauty of utterance was surely enough, I thought I had read this.
A wind rose as I tore out my ravishing tenor, or sank down to throb
on my pitted hindquarters while my neck with its primrose striations
pulsated and gleamed. Then beauty sobbed back to me, shocking,
its counterpoint catching my harmonies; I had heard a fresh voice.

8

No longer alone, not espousing Narcissus, I answered each peal
in a drum of delirium, recalling with shame the dry white thighs
of frogs like baked chicken wishbones, sorely in need of a sauce.
Our calls clasped in common, as heavy as love, and convulsively
thickened by love – until ashamed of such ordinariness, I wailed
in sheer vowels. Aaghoooh, I sloughed off raark, aaarrgh noises,
deliberately degenerate; exuded ooeeehaargh-I-oohyuuuh; then
randomly honked 'darkling blue of Dimitrios': I had dreamed that.

9

The voice hears itself as it sings to its fellows – must
thrum in its own ears, like any noise thumping down
anywhere airwaves must equably fall. I was not that
Narcissus who stared stunned by his handsomeness;
or I was, but not culpably, since as I sang, so I loved.
In that action of calling hope out I embodied it, grew
solemn and swollen ushering in my own utterance.
I rang florid yet grave in my ears, as I had to.

o

Did I need to account for myself as noise-maker?
I had stared in the windows of Clerkenwell clock shops
at dusty brand oils for the watchmakers' trade, made for
easing the wound spring – some *horo*-prefixed, and so close
to my horror of time ticking by – brown bottles of clock oil
labelled Horolene, Horotech. Should I wind up my own time,
chant 'I was dropped on the Borders, a poor scraplet of
Langholm, illegit. and state's burden, lone mother of three'?

1

Could I try on that song of my sociologized self? Its
long angry flounce, tuned to piping self-sorrow, flopped
wax in my gullet – 'But we're all *bufo bufo*,' I sobbed –
suddenly charmed by community – 'all warty we are.'
Low booms from the blackness welled up like dark liquid
of 'wart' Ich auf Dich'. One Love was pulsed out from our
isolate throats, concertinaed in common; 'Du mit Mir' was
a comforting wheeze of old buffers, all coupled, one breed.

2

But then I heard others, odd pockets of sound; why wouldn't these
claim me to chant in their choir? As I grew lonelier I got philosophical
and piped up this line: 'Don't fall for paradox, to lie choked in its coils
while your years sidle by.' Some hooted reproachfully out of the dawn
'don't *you* stifle *us* with your egotist's narrative or go soft on "sameness",
we'll plait our own wildly elaborate patterns' – they bristled like movies
Kurosawa. By then I'd re-flated, abandoned my toadhood, had pulled
on my usual skin like old nylons. I drifted to Delphi, I'd a temple
to see.

Puff

True sweetness must fan out to find its end
but tied off from its object it will swell –

lumping across sterile air it counts itself
lonely and brave. At once it festers. Why shape

these sentiments, prosecution witnesses, in violet
washes of light where rock cascades to water bluer

than powdering hopes of home. A hook's tossed out
across one shoulder to snag on to any tufts of thrift:

have I spoken only when things have hardened?
But wouldn't the fact of you melt a watch?

Unfurls no father-car umbrella here. No beautiful
fate is sought, nor any cut-out heart renunciation

– if only some Aztec god could get placated! But he don't –
there's just a swollen modesty to champ at its own breast.

High on itself, it sings of its own end, rejoicing
that this cannot come about. Because I am alive here.

So Is It?

Opening mouth up to sifting rain, blurred to an o,
crouched to the green wash, swooping water,
stone arches slit to wind-cropped turf, in a grip
turn as sea-slicing gannets cut shock fans of
white water. Held shudder, sluiced in low cloud.
Where is a steady place where work gets fairly done.
Straight speech can drop out from behind the teeth
or the hands shake out clean strokes from bunched
knots onto energetic white or long soft ropes of
line loop from the mouth, uncoil to columns
hollowed to poured sheen purity, only in shelter.
Some. I walk into a light hot wood. Inside it all
exhales, a sulky wind gets up, slings a sad mass
at the back of eyes lowered for chattering dusk,
fingers dried ochres in rough air brushed rustling
to cream hoops, strokes powdery blues tacked on
to black wire. Die deeper into life at every second.
And no self coating slips onto my papers to make
them pulse to rooms emptied of me, they'll bear no
faint film for my children to wipe off later, so solidly
do objects stay themselves – the handwriting of the
freshly dead just doesn't get any loopier or more
archaic, as waxed comb honey would seep through
knuckles or pine ooze stiffen, domed to wasps.
Things packed with what they are. Not slatted I.
Preserve a self, for what? for ice through the ribs,
pale splinters driven straight to the heart's meat.
Calf of my senses. I'd thought out ways to grasp –
have walked straight off their edges. To dreams

of silent towns, nights, doorways, gazes, radios
on, while here a man turns and turns towards his
window, staring out over the street at dusk as rain-
hemmed curtains sway, their blackening yellowed
net. All seek a piercing charm to throb gingerly
nursed in our hands like a bird. Dear heart don't be
so strange to me but be nature. Or give me a sudden
bluish look. If I can get this far. An oil spill on the
wet road swims outwards, pleats, and flashes lilac or
rusting orange at its rim where it will dry and darken.
I think that's it. As I must think it is like this for you –
it is, isn't it. Don't tell me that edge that I never believe.

Dark Looks

Who anyone is or I am is nothing to the work. The writer
properly should be the last person that the reader or the listener need
   think about
yet the poet with her signature stands up trembling, grateful, mortally
   embarrassed
and especially embarrassing to herself, patting her hair and twittering
   'If, if only
I need not have a physical appearance! To be sheer air, and mousseline!'
and as she frets the minute wars scorch on through paranoias of the
   unreviewed
herded against a cold that drives us in together – then pat me more,
   Coventry
to fall from anglo-catholic clouds of drifting *we*'s high tones of feeling
   down
to microscopic horror scans of tiny shiny surfaces rammed up against
   the nose
cascading on Niagara, bobbed and jostled, racing rusted cans of Joseph
   Cotten reels
charmed with his decent gleam: once *we* as incense-shrouded ectoplasm
   gets blown
fresh drenched and scattered units pull on gloss coats to preen in their
   own polymer:
still it's not right to flare and quiver at some fictive 'worldly boredom
   of the young'
through middle-aged hormonal pride of *Madame, one must bleed, it's
   necessary* . . .
The only point of holding up my blood is if you'd think 'So what?
We've all got some of that': since then you'd each feel better; less apart.
   – Hardly:

it's more for me to know that *I* have got some, like a textbook sexual
   anxiety
while the social-worker poet in me would like her revenge for having
   been born and left.
What forces the lyric person to put itself on trial though it must stay
   rigorously uninteresting?
Does it count on its dullness to seem human and strongly lovable; a
   veil for the monomania
which likes to feel itself helpless and touching at times? Or else it backs
   off to get sassy
since arch isn't far from desperate: So take me or leave me. No, wait,
   I didn't mean leave
me, wait, just *don't* – or don't flick and skim to the foot of a page and
   then get up to go –

Disintegrate Me

There was such brilliance lifting off the sea, its aquamarine strip
blocked in behind white-dashed mimosas, that it stung my eyes
all morning as I stood in the old playground, pushing the swing
steadily, looking out across the water and longing to do without
these radio voices, and without my post as zealous secretary, as
transmitter of messages from the dead, who'd issue disclaimers
that they'd ever sent them – all the while a slow hot cut spreads
to baste me now with questions of my own complicity in harm
muttering thoughtfully about 'patterns' until I'm stamped out as
an old paisley shawl or worn kelim, do I look good as this one
or should I be less loud or less repetitive? and on the top of my
wardrobe, familiar spirits cluster and hang to chatter, lean over
to peer down interestedly at me, vivaciously complaining about
the large amounts of fluff I've left up there, 'that's just as we'd
expect': meanwhile the out-to-kill person is not, or so she or he
shrugs, pulled at by voices, but dead at heart stands amnesiac
plumped out with the effective innocence of the untroubled –
This gloss is taking me on unconvincing dashes down blind
alleys I mistrust, since desperate to see things straight I can't fit
apt blame in to self-damnation: could I believe instead in drained
abandon, in mild drift out over some creamy acre studded with
brick reds, to be lifted, eased above great sienna fields and born
onward to be an opened stem or a standing hollow, a flesh ring
through which all slips or a fluent cylinder washed through by
azure-tangled braid, trailing Stella Maris, fervent star of the sea
marine milk vessel flopped at the lip, flicking down swathes of
gulls emulsifying blackened earth striped and coiled under rock
under burnt straw air fuzzed in breathy fields of coconut-sharp
gorse flowers flushed tan on cliffs where lower toothpaste-green

lucidly rears and rears to the crash of blinding crumpled water
smoothing to clear and flat; so calmly let me disperse so simply
let me disperse drawn out thin-frothed in a broad lacy pancake
fan of salt, or let me fall back as dolphins rock back in the sea
twirled like slow toys on pin-wheels – No single word of this
is any more than decoration of an old self-magnifying wish
to throw the self away so violently and widely that interrogation
has to pause since its chief suspect's sloped off to be cloud, to be
wavery colour bands: no 'release from service to a hard master'
said of the thankful close, it's hoped, of sexual need in oldest age
can touch this other drive of shame fighting to clear a name to itself:
it can't, because its motor runs on a conviction that if I understood
my own extent of blame then that would prove me agent: it doesn't
want to face a likely truth of helplessness – that the inflated will to
gauge and skewer each wrong turn may blank out what's far worse
to bear: impersonal hazard, the humiliating lack of much control –
I don't get past this thought with any confidence.

Shantung

It's true that anyone can fall
in love with anyone at all.
Later, they can't. Ouf, ouf.

How much mascara washes away each day
and internationally, making the blue one black.
Come on everybody. Especially you girls.

Each day I think of something about dying.
Does everybody? do they think too, I mean.
My friends! some answers. Gently
unstrap my wristwatch. Lay it face down.

Iain Sinclair

a bull called remorse

either nude and pulled behind as well as
fixed in plucking mud, an anchor
to his own need, as the Silurian effluent
scums to the surface in
a vortex of jaw-defying squidmeat

'elegant,' says the child, meaning the opposite
and accurate to the last spasm

scraping sunwounds from the salmon
the adrenalin releasing warts of
dried mushroom a flashback
film death, dyed in the Sixties,
red paint hair – the tribesman cannot
write himself back into his last scenario

present in a wholly alien period he hopes
to find the lock that his special interest deformities
can enter, he is alone and singular

all hooks out, defenceless
two salt channels of information
pitting his tangerine cheeks

with Madame Thatcher
'I've had to learn to carve meat'

hence, like foxes

as unlikely as 'Canadian Pataphysics'
heat, that lovely (block) word
that can so easily be placed alongside
simple terms such as 'Big' or 'White'
and impersonated by Lee Marvin or
a robot version, less complicated
but more enthusiastic than the original

guardian police with faces
like their own helmets hotwire representational
Rovers (the colour of dogsick), haul 'em off
spray-shirted, chisel peak hair, built
around ginger moustaches, quiet fans
of the simplest solution, polishing
our kidneys with soft boots

riotous streets out of control when
a dazzling blonde is hallucinated without
underwear by a stoop of panting stationer's assistants
a smoking lounge of horseflesh punters

all sublimate erections into truncheons
and back again – streetlife
gets stickier by the hour (Sandringham Road)

longing for darkness when the blunted leaves
split and spill their poultice of black juices

and we dream of travelling oaks
the freedom to move in the excrement of birds

97

german bite

for Gerry Goldstein

an excitement of 'too much'

the hands of the junkie not
as spectacular as the hands of Orlac
but as much of a functioning instrument
guiding the hit into what's left
of the thinking machine

as if talking could be anything more than talking
the world unsettled and not remade

too many reports of books telephones visions
explaining the Usury Theory while
eagerly demonstrating it

blood under the skin, paper dirt on it

talking with carolyn

I am starting sax lessons in September . . .
Psychoanalysis follows in October.
                                          – Neal Cassady

dusted in unexceptional manuscripts

the truth that was and
is now an over-applied cosmetic:
eyelashes cut from flea combs

tho' still capable on parting, a touch
ring hand to shoulder

as if comrades in a revolution
that had been decisively defeated

talking with our brains cut out
shocked to be lifted
from the safety of myth

a hat thrown in the air, a leg that's lost

An honest woman breaks her leg at home.
                              – Luis Buñuel

trust is a meadow the light in my eyes
a peculiar opacity, fearing blindness
and surprise itself the source of fear

honouring the mortar the ditch
in photographs that remain potential

the whistle of an arrow or the bark of a dog
hearing in images the ear has a greater
depth of field and what it cannot fix
goes back into the shawl of darkness

better to exercise your fingers across the tabletop
than mutilate a televised sonata

dream is serial like *The Vengeance of Fu Manchu*,
not episodic, each sequence having
the same weight the same structure, a pornography
of gesture not action

asleep in the armchair, but
not yet become it, solitude crystallizes
like wax fruit in a golden bowl

                                        Framlingham
                                        30 October 1983

serpent to zymurgy

more diseases than textbooks

I had thought St Vitus's dance as much
of a back number as the cakewalk ;
it's stomping here in full fig
velveteen jacket worn to flesh, pocket
torn out, split like a chicken carcass

try and lift from the coop
of Old Holborn phlegm twitch
parrot moods – they've even
picked up on bird diseases & foul pests

the lolling, sheepheaded beaten
men, the form filling
dole-scratching, ill-tempered
mess of what we have become

this post office has more patients
than a surgery, sliding
up to the re-taped window across
a gob-spattered stone floor

on the low parapet wall of the flats
some wasted jailbait perfectly imitates
the ka-aar of the shiteating seagull

ka-aar, ka-aar, ka-aar
wait long enough
and the roles will be painlessly reversed

street detail

his bare arm a gold box
on the roof of the Jag,
at the lights and then

having to flick the box
into the street not
breaking off his talk

For Sale notice, phone
number on rear ledge

you don't
stuff the packet
back through a window
of that vintage

old-style, smoking villains

autistic poses

Alive, but past recall.

her heels worn raw
two bacon-coloured patches
(dollar sized)

black crombie
collar turned up &
covered in white dog hairs

'I haven't been well'

damp snuffling ahead,
dry rasping cough behind

the shopping precinct
vanishes into a glass screen:

This safe has a Time Delaying lock

our official no brahmin
low caste as a cricket umpire
shovels out reluctant benefits

on his wall a map of London
cut off at the Thames
so that the south
is not merely *terra incognita*

it doesn't exist

hurricane drummers: self-aid in haggerston

Ronnie Kray is now in Broadmoor and brother Reggie in Parkhurst
from where he is trying . . . to get a security firm called Budrill off the
ground.

there's a mob of rumours from s. of the river
challenging the teak and shattering glass
with dropkicks honed on GLC grant aid – Nike soles
stamp out likely prints of light, moth-shaped entries

another team of semi-skilled dips work
the precinct, dry cleaning my credits my
licences and small wad of royal portraits
allowing them to collect on unconvincing promises

a couple of vehicles are cased
and a couple elbowed

in reply the locals can offer
a squadcar of handy lads looking for lefty,
cruising on new rubbers that
give the game away, authentic
as any red light disco chuck-outs

employment prospects are good
for the wolf importers the cross-
breeders of beasts with more
jaw than brain – the bells! the bells!

charm out in celebration,
aerobic heels flash high torsion
round the corner of Queensbridge Road

'hey, what is it about this place?'
says the reverend suddenly
looking out of the window at
a group of black youths as we
approach Dalston.
'they're smoking reefer on the street!'

'music is music,' says Cleveland,
returning to the subject.
'it's the words that separates
gospel from the rest. only the words.'

in the latest proof of ackroyd

1/4 inch to the W. of
'fibres, hair, ash, burnt paper'
a small insect has died

4 legs attached, the fifth
and sixth a mere stain

their substance on the opposite page,
solitary, 1/4 inch to the E. of

'disconcerted Hawksmoor. He
called for a roll of adhesive tape'

kristallnacht

When Soutine finally consulted an ear specialist about the terrible ear-
ache, in the canal of the painter's ear the doctor discovered, not an
abscess but a nest of bedbugs.

escape with the children but
escape them we cannot, will not
draw up beyond this breath:
beeswax burning in an old tin cup

break the ring with
a child's soft head before
it's too late, it is
already, cold fear

a glove turned, waxy smoke
boiled honey evoking
a woman's blood string, does not arouse

it terrifies us and the protection
which is this room marked
with its square posts becomes
a place of torment – the children
we discover in ourselves are

drained, stars
on the curve of their lids

the unfocused night
runs wild as a scalded dog

significant wreckage

The isle is full of noises.

I

the Turk sent his catamite swimming to shore
in quest of one perfect juice-tight grape
salt-stiff lips, skin torn on thorn, crazy
sandstone profiles in the cliff, returned
all risks cancelled in this violation,
a broken branch – burnt alive, barbecued
on the hillside the smoke visible
a mile out, across tame, shaming water

when the statues walked I slept
and could not move so set
that muscles confined in plaster seemed wet:
a low sleep that presses an imprint of
breath's fern into a chalkwhite ceiling

these moulded angels cradle the instruments
that cut them free from an account of life:
the skinner's blade, the sharktooth saw,
the adze – paleness is excused, boiled
in olive oil, rashered, peeled or dropped in pans

each village celebrates its own translation
a mute in the tower slams the clapper
rocking the skirted bell in which he squats
and flies are the knots that have escaped

a wall of disease mementoes rags
bandages crutches photographs that
swallow all the taint of fever to age
in a dream of dim sepsis, privileged pain

the accusing fingers, the supplicating bones
are snapped, lost from the path
evolve to lizards or to gecko life
escape the station, abrupt as fretted cocks

words wriggle in a heat that
slides them from the sugar'd page
the saint becomes a lectern to
the truth — unburied, a newborn
nakedness, fish naked, not unclothed

break them with hammers they yield
no word, heartless untongued:
villagers recage their passions
and their flaws, no need
to stave the pirates or to choke the well

stoic they watch
death tighten the web, not grow
skin for aboriginal flight, a chill ledge
for the griddled sun

2

swimming the salt and sticky with pearls
glove fish, you are trapped in an abstract
of grace, float the world, glazed to a curve,
sky free, unclouded: rock cave, alder copse

it folds as legend, is recalled:
the candle flame, detached from its lard,
under hot ground — black mushroom cap
our guide, his damaged recitative

(the primal version is untold
but flares in flashlit eyes, a panic red!)

figs burst between your fingers
the island is barren in its dust and flags:
they lift blind saints onto their pedestals with
swaying cranes, deafen them with thunderflashes

brotherhood of marching bands and shirts that
are too tight, secret signs – the police
in black glasses, guns; barebreasted
a German bitch under the Christ stack, crones
mutter, pull knuckles; lovers wrestle
in mannerless surf, disgendered, scapegoat

3

travesties of dwarf strength, they scale
cane ladders with cheese-stone blocks
cutting into their shoulders – the White Goddess
is in death drag, red mouthed, spitting out
pomegranate seeds, split figs, hair

the island shield is lit by blades, rubric
of skulls and incense, faked bells
confessions broadcast to the wind

a heresy of beards restages all
the cultic feasts, migrant birds
are netted, overcooked, the wine
is scented, peeling teeth

principality of hills dogs stars
a place to quit, the circuit of the sea
erases pique: juniper logs and cedarwood

in catalogue fresh ruins, the amphitheatre
of some discharged Herod, we sit
beneath a rage of crucified leper waxworks,
our backs turned away from
a dark feathering of smoke blown seawards

San Lawrenz, Gozo
1987

jack elam's other eye

that black psychosis which many psychoanalysts now assume lies at
the base of consciousness

letter never sent, of things you didn't see
the pheasant outside my leaking keyhole
bright beak & wobbly neck, always stiff tail
associated with the verb 'kill', & next
the sharpened fin of rock they call
'black', from which it is not easy
to spot the secret ruins of the abbey,
the trout pond or the tree

(even sympathetic natives give these a miss)

single-bar electric fire, embroidered cushion-
bird, black & white tv, not
fearing the dust-mouthed presence that
is forever here; more, much more
than my telling of it, speaking aloud
is all I have to say: a bell

enclosed in a slatted turret, a hump of grass
less real than the watercolours on the wall

only *then* will we know what confinement means

scraps & green heaps

wie anders sei noch geschlafen als stehend
— Paul Celan

opposite the scrapyard & across the river
we were walking apart but calmly
in the same direction, shingle, noise linked
the anger of a spurned machine a moveable grab
producing nothing more than a satisfied crunch
digested automobiles cancelled traffic the threat
disturbed your sense of occasion hardly at all

the few yards of clear sand a finite
shelf of pebbled eggs fragments of green glass
well worth the picking over & thus
too far beyond our means

losing sight of the river itself
stoking our appetites on a crust
of pink fishmeat blue oil
smoke persuaded from a lettuce leaf

no call to go further & we came back
well over the limit a sidelong glance
at the morbid stalk of Canary Wharf

then at it like a whole tray of bright cutlery
exploiting opportunity metal buffers clanging
in appreciation of the hurricane's diminishment

want it enough & you can, have it all

recovery & death

late daisies, burnt leaves
curling at the edges
in currents of moist air

patched skin from whose face
whose eyes?

the silver sun stirs a high tumbler
a pool among the tree tops

LEON is a TRAMP.
And his mother is a slag.
And she wears shit shoes
that cost £1.99p

a bench that is not designed for rest
his back to the scene he is barely describing

Victoria Park
13 October 1988

pogrom music

Armageddon, with mirrors.

the aniline dye travels faster than my will permits
slides dutiful penetrates the targeted source of
unlicensed growth proud to glow
in negative plates orthodox heresies oppulent tissue
must yield to the district's blade: cut clean, rubbished burnt

& the sun proceeds unmoved among cirric threads
passing through fixed points as on the thong
that held Apollinaire's shattered skull in place not
quite in time closing on
the immaculate balance of Christ Church tower

at length warm a private place easy
among roofs slates slatboard shifts
they frame a patch of sunlight & innocently
fan motes empty as the *Angelus* stain
now shocked blitz wallpaper hears
the wooden pace the rabbi & his daughter dividing
the ceiling over balconies of memorial art

defend yourself in childbirth or split
like a red pomegranate 'your voice . . . our deacon'
sudden mosses cold sharp pools revealed among the boards
the shadow a potential man making his curse
forbidding the future
that has prematurely surveyed his corkscrewed bones

logging the debris of unrecorded necks & ties
a room suffers more to be returned
than ever it can grant in recompense

nothing to falsify the register of ruin whose cities
are already known & therefore damned in carbon dust

all we transcribe is a mute affection

maldor furs

midnight daughters splice the lemon summons
herded together in salt baths eager to answer
(who calls & who remembers)

let the empty picture book flick
on a scrubbed oak table the steppe wind
seems the only *rational* explanation &
surely least worthy to nominate

the devil's teat
growing from the side of my finger

nil by mouth

among the unfumigated lungs of the poor
naked ears unboiled
brazen hoops piercing thin cartilage
as they plod towards allowance pension virgin cash
bang goes the punch promises promises
shuffle in on themselves the glass
next one elbows forward in case
it should all turn out to be exactly what it is
just another paper fraud

(are Lee Harwood's clients anything like this?)

wanting a mere stamp to ship a book
seems decadent & extreme
lives of the not quite desperate ourselves
coughing the dust of official sanction
too far gone to appreciate
the counter clerk's excessive shirt
John Cage doodles scoring the chorus
gobbing sputum expulsion
the dim the dull the reversed scene

necks of knotted flesh horsetail hair
tied with silly rags the only place
where there is world enough to write

chernobyl priests

there is no death in us we are all sick
the electric typewriter rattles like a dying spasm
life being unzipped from a gashed throat
a white fishbone cutting flesh a hedge strimmer

fallen out from gravity of love to travel
solitary in straight lines tracked
by what we are tracking the silverside
train of fate the sealed express
that does not appear to suffer or to move

children raising khaki sheets to their lips
old women at prayer perched along the sill
heated until they crack the varnish splits

in prolonged silence the pastry sinks
a pie of bandages or sheep escape the pot
spilling earth & pellets of grey dung

aslant the parquet an impact of sand a desert
nobody dares protected blocks infirm terrain
sunbathers nude among the smoking ruins
where official portraits used to hang &
who now will nominate the photographs to burn

gin had no connection with time

out of the cloister the poetry reading fugitive faces
'wind down your window please sir'
the parked car, as Patrick notes, files our registration
he also had something to say about those pillars
petering out in an unashamed absence of meaning
a folded heap of laundry well-ironed convict shirts

it is always the one with the rimless spectacles who
gets to speak – *Girton or the Crematorium?*
we'll never it's true in this life achieve
Ian Patterson's house not on this weary circuit

we pound the Bateman & the Panton streets our heads
bereft of numbers even try one door, 45, to honest
incredulity – 'the poet preaches as a silk of silver'
threads a discourse a cape reversed his audience
cavort in joy to hear confirmed what they always knew

(&, coughing, the outsize essayist quits the salon
to eavesdrop at a distant door)

we are all here make of our congregation
what you will, the greyhead the woman
in a boy's pink sweater, the lovers of truth

but this stuff has become so *peculiar*
there's no audience for it no reader
imagine that, good, the ideal reader who will never,
thank god, step forward to declare herself

it hurts, only women know
there is still some centre that might work
& do not refuse to shout for it or sing

the carnal gate: hitman in a private garden

as the circuit of the garden is an oval sentence
with its staging posts pets' graveyard draw breath
sit on the wet slats of a white bench
celebrating a spring shower or the gardener's hose
when a climax of meaning tips the alcove news of
Charlie 'The Silent Man' Wilson already cooking the trumpet
spitting scarlet rumours across poplin sheets how
a 'pale youth' rang the anniversary bell to gain access
walked him out towards the lapping pool intent
on a bit of business landed first a sneaky blow
side of the nose knee'd him in the groin with enough force
to show up on the pathologist's report eased
the oiled barrel intimately against or into his mouth &
blew away the roof of his skull

Henry James' holograph tended to droop
towards the margin black ink revisions
the famous library regathered I can't recall
a kinder evening setting sun over the red roofs
English ladies counting coin fearing a present absence
I strolled without knowledge Charlie
would be cremated along with a dog won
in a poker game their sympathetic ashes mingled

when my father's blue pen pressed to service
gave up the ghost I changed hands reaching
into the drawer the slim silver affair my wife gave me
again picking up the original a posthumous spurt
as if the balled nib had merely *debated* its rapid passage
the resistant grease of the notebook's lined page
a mortal strain trembling through my arm

Lamb House, Rye
29 April 1990

the shaman's pouch

unyielding, the pliancy of
night's sprung ribs

from which we build
a darkness where nothing lives

and life is felt & fur & brine

Isle of Harris
19 January 1991

boat dresses

for Steve & Joan Dilworth

whiskey & flakes of green leaf,
fish oil, pink stone meat
spilling its lucid fat

        a lung feather in the throat
        breaks the tarpaulin,
        sorrow of a buried wing

death is an easier thing,
black water nights
pressing moisture from the moor's bones

        leave now, left ticking
        out, beyond the graveyard's sand

a chest of swords, a dying tree
an empty church, a spear cage

        the vertical narrative
        of unchanging names

camera obscura

for the author of The Stumbling Block

lepidopterist of memory, of ice. erasure, the road
bone chants, moustaches wet with yak butter. glacial debris
in your slack mouth. a lost tooth susurrates

pink blood on the outhouse wall he
passes childhood, dreads to hear truth's lure
or: wire slices her lip with 'heavy duty' blade

we live in sound retrace the rasp of curses
carbon breath lifting paper from a dying eye. love
in a jar. things happen often & again.

as milk to mercy runs the disks you name
are anklebones, a pendulum of hazard. scarlet insects
shrieking in a clock. sheathed fingers tapping final storms

now lightning reverie speaks, approaching core.
bruises in transition spit venom, lily pads.
a whiskey bottle is seen as a swallowed telescope

father's throat opened to surgical intervention
essence of brass, goldwatch gobbed against the abused
lid of an Hasidic trilby in a cobbled lane.

tabled on microphone altar painted revelations
broadcast a city's silence. taboo of candlefat
dew of sexual transmission. the bench of paradox

friendly fire

better yet to wander the town
than rest my cheek on the desk's varnished surface
hair cracks, skull cracks, acid stains
book-cleaning operations
better the flight the sweating cloth the map
screwed under your armpit
like a rivet, a conquered bubo

break the curse of inscription
driftwater oilswell tarpaulin
the hard circumference of dream erasure

it's only by report that I screamed in the night
if it wasn't for a bent horizon
the hair-fine twitching of the black upper
branches the soot hangovers

I'd be mad as a crow, axle-slick'd
with bloody gobbets in my teeth &
dog excrement coating my lips
& speaking tediously in formal iron

new nights, lights beyond interpretation
railway barracks hissing platforms
where ice trains stall for want of paper

not even, not ever, not now
having to write ourselves out of the story

immaculate corruptions

i.m. AC

'boiled cabbage & gin hanging in the air'
bird-skid, delayed nostalgia of heavy plant
essays a thin arterial road, Cambridge
and The North . . .

black stockings, kites upstairs
mature fright wig doubling for
the Infant mistress hurrying home

I refuse the play of reflections
in the portrait glass, light from outside.
ceramic steam, all the dark truth
that shades your profile in the reeve
of our child's sunburst head

a bright slate roof where
indifferently the vanished cat
the wasps & broken coffee bowl
will always endure

sanctuary knocker

The only respect in which he was a Christian was the interest he shared
with Christ in professional women.

– Edward Dorn

the telephone rests on Swedenborg (Yeats too &
WH Hodgson, the *Master Map of London*)
lunch booked in the revamped chophouse better days known
less on the table costing more the borderline dyke she
says she's been sick for months City within a city
the holy well, well yes, we'll all be dead soon
has any one single human body survived
they've jawed about it certainly brushed vine chalk from
their shoulders their hair the former
novelist wants to try ladies' clothes wants
rephrase that to talk about drink
time curdling like a refulgent turd one Bruce
Chatwin forgot to shoot beside the desert road
uncensored censoring things a sharp pain in the neck
inherited from a Mortlake gravestone not one sentient being
on this planet knows who Helen Redpath was

a group of men, all called john

mid-afternoon: lazy bars
across undip'd headlights,
a red Jag 4.2 against a green pub

& WC Williams is *still* dead

precious & straw

the whistle of the cat-catcher in the night
the native Londoner with his wriggling sack
his plunder hair & fogged skin
pouching grey laurel lint
keeping the craft tradition (severed hand) alive

20,000 books feed on the barber's lungs
a stall aborts his son's display
coal beach, half-hunters shovelled onto felt

damp mortar, creamstone hedge
lost documentation expelling verse

where the talent is

i.m. Derek Raymond

sweating bread
Colombian coffee fires tongue & date
the cheap watch clicks lunchhour
pushing the scribe towards a hard-earned amnesiac seizure
hot as the thought of hell:
keys, fever beads
we send for Polaroids to confirm our loss

the symbol in the cemetery avenue
overreaches itself lacks sap in the vein
Herne horns of living ash better far
to visit the site than to have it described

that which appears

as old men dancing return sap to the springboard
not needing nor wanting, not needing
the bank's yellow blood, earth scalded in water

so far beyond the rule of zero
(footpath closed by criminals with faded ribbons)
to set a water-compass at true north & zip it
securely inside the flap of a sheepskin bag before
renting a surrogate to forget the whole matter

'off to the Orkneys in small stages'
read the suicide note of Cynthia Nolan

more kissing than teaching

cinema flag (on a clean white pole)
an American breakfast:
'The Gateway to the Cotswolds'

revenge of the river horse

I celebrate the loss of rain
losing outside sounds that fret on glass
thin as a membrane dividing that
which is not to be known from all the rest

sliding slipping following
the stream down the mountain
vertical excited strokes a pigeon hook
shaped in steel to caress
the coldness of your back the cancer-
granting, cancer-saving fern:
View from the Gantry
slate bright as moonlight on coal
wise children conceived in porcelain tubs

the spokes of an upturned bicycle
hum at the bedside
in a reviving, prophylactic hymn

no saddle no reprieve
black fly-breath of a snipered mule

travellers by appointment only

the leaves are heavy as wet skin
and suicide is the hook in the throat
(one & only one)
a mad person unsexed in her shout
unwilling to vanish she sticks
like the stink of your best friend's shit
sprayed from an aerosol to offend
a cornershop that defies geometry by
standing at the awkward centre of the triangle

so swiftly the shirt rushes forward
not refusing cigarette custom
greeting it instead with a fumigation brand

fuck, fuck the words we can't quite
hear, china gums bared, black cavity
she plunges headlong skating
on cones of steaming dog dirt, one slipper
privates sluiced at a public tap

read my lisp

let the crows with their cutpurse habits
              have it
the air the oily grass & all the meat
the city spits out – let them kaw
mobhanded, gorblimey & selfish as
old hoods, memory thieves in
apple-green rooms obliging history
let crows expose themselves in bare trees
fat as gristle kebabs
& louder than something you
bite alive

'let him have it chris'

colourless light the blue bomber cap
on the balcony the ape-fit
pensioner who used to lift shirts
a solitary brylcream dog
abusing shelves tastes his ink-
newspaper with uncivil tongue

it's our town the crows know that
chalk worms in the starry ground under
a hung carpet of clystered smoak

window watches

heart as silent as the Swatch is loud
(the curse of documentary crews)
pigeon shadows less than three frames across
the brick screen, wet slates where
frost's confectionery has failed – write if you must
but still you're deader than when you started this

I have paperback books instead
of perfectly glossy envelopes of salt
I have commissions instead of
emissions that would empty the pouch
& give it a chance to restock
darkness blue as spider ink

I have a warrant made out in the wrong name

I know who edits the *Independent*'s obituary column
but I don't know when

blind mendoza's saucer

in the oyster bars shells
fill with borrowed hair, so track
the taste an unsuspected trip –
lefthand spiral to flatter the dome
lick out lardmeat & avoid
the drop: satin thong silk mosaic
home for tv, clergy. orange
2-bar fizzing like corncobs
wedged in the cheek. *yes sah boss.*
morningside grin & coiffured flick
that costs more than decommissioning
a presidential Boeing. bombers
pick up hefty credit spreading oil &
flesh across the battery-lit snow

vibrating finger deletes the dusty screen

insomnia

a man can fall backwards from a window
& live or die according to the requirements of the script
& it can happen in the Renoir Bloomsbury
or the Arts Cinema Cambridge
but the coat in question, the black slicker, vanishes forever
'you're wearing my stuff'

unable to sleep I read William Burroughs'
book of dreams (a lie)
unable to sleep I write, unable to sleep
I read William Burroughs' book of dreams
(not true) thinking of Catherine Blake who
sat for hours beside her husband
whose 'inspirations' threatened to 'tear him asunder'
graved voices of retrospective prophecy

recovered from suburban flicks, we applaud
'a young PT instructor shooting rats with an air-rifle'

the missing hyphen of *Stumbling Block*
the proof of that curious name, Kells Elvins
the dry boast: 'bring me a leper & I will kiss it'

the ebbing of the kraft

The only English word I knew was 'yes'.
            – Willem de Kooning

like a butcher I relish the drive to work
poplars primed with glycerine
who needs to observe the stealth of nature
cathedral icehouse where all hats are white &
regimental crombies crack like sodden wood
drying out in a tax inspector's office.
the kill is stockings & meat. hanged buds
in wild orchards where children
scrump for soap.
taps run blood to wash away the water
our road is clean as best linen. in the old house
with its marsh-gas boiler a wife
distempers what I leave behind, strapped
gloves on which the wool still grows
blackberries to spit on pristine sheets

as wait you must for the summoned stranger
the mannerless oak

'the dove which is brought back to life by the hawk'

homage to the roebuck

so much can be said when the walls are left
standing by themselves revealed at last
the secret no longer worth the keeping old man
enlightened suspicious of the son holding down
that mortem of history – dust
instead of air. cancel the stench of
the leashed dog its brute circumference, apron & spike
no ice in the bucket no purple heel to sip
the site is a film of powdered stone
brought to ground,
a gesture of unmindful erasure
bones dance against the wall
their crime is longer than their life
shadows driven underground
a river of lost voices
the beast in the thicket curious
about the split prism the star-burst
newsflash of the hunter's rifle

angrave passage

language was a thirsty coat
beneath heavy damask
tassels come to their first grey screen
a toasted wafer in the colour field
a rein of disrobed talk the way
tent folk shouted praise
– creeping, curdled, sad
not I who raised the french maid's skirt
or prised a tile, knowing her brief
was eternity no less knowing meat
the stink of steaming sprouts in a pressure pan
crawling down the ledge, older
& safer than the lesser dead, refusing to learn
what they were incapable of leaving behind

paradise row

hang-loose journos decanting stateside
with cash pillows that painters could usefully burn
an advertised woman's hairshirt & pubic extensions
topiarize her muff to a pink wembley heart

the deal lacks food the laptop dancer
takes too much on herself can't
read the plaintiff's mind (his regal quiff)

auteurs étrangers & folk who live in exile
without knowing it feel at home
wherever they trull from a foreign bed,
Menilmontant light from the cemetery wall

catch it before it unrolls
like a carpet underlay & the phone
shrills to query its suspect documentation

glibbery electrical

Looking back, my throat has always been my Achilles heel.
                                                    – Jacqueline Bisset

lightblue shoulder bands against a wet pink door
the immutable flat cap & hands in leisure wear
each day, key in lock, nowhere special to go
shop sold shop closed Parkinson's disease
(& Parkinson doesn't want it anymore)
back home with a soggy roll of newsprint
confirming the worst, implants blessed
with qualities beyond description, balcony life
to shelf life, living too far from the deck old creeper

1½ tablets of something like Prozac
as *digestif* of choice after 3 or more solid pints
greenish white the boy
buggered on the lavatory's checkerboard floor, not worth
the call out the dull & dusty wind
ambulances that lose their way across the marshes

returns opens his hutch enters
leaves again almost immediately, the elaborate
pantomime of the lock-up, spying out the ledge
strangling his string dog with public love

hot food brings news of fear in foil trays
airline scoff for those who do not travel
dramatic fissure of the medial ligaments as
everything above the palate dries in sympathy

wreaths in the doorway, Bancroft Road coral
unexplained ballast discovered on foreshore
all fruit & flesh sucked off by water

move out, move on, move fast

bath wife steel teeth

exhaustion. cep. mauve dill
Sag Harbor oven mothers who trail film curl
blackskin tails from hellmouth (enamel)
the fat of spit.
white lead fruit. lemonwash as
spite. the letter *d* (no apostrophe). sap
orange pulp. new pope's squeeze. roe
in a tube. tubular paste
razor red. enough muscle in play
to get it done fast. to read as
it comes back on itself.
thermometer skirt hem flap
he says let it alone he says
steepling waves overwhelm, whelp
can't quit can't. into feather (pile)
into split pulse. give her give her
the bonus bed. yes the quilt of dough flesh

sub (not used): Mountain

prize cicatrix suspended in oil
charts flapping proud from damp walls
which are themselves charts
of islands where swamps are undeclared
the superseded house
brutish topiary of the illegitimate bride
weather systems registering a pigeon shed
my lord at his grouse table
filing his second rank of teeth
will you risk the caretaker's gamey tape
the black worm that lives reluctant in altar bread
an hermaphroditic pope whose lard fingers
slip their rings

strapped into rented ligatures
he stomps the town
dragging Kent & all her oasts behind him

egg rolling in a stone age culture

atrophy of idiolect
atrophy of pearls & peaches
steam on the cusp of your brandy balloon
brandy from a sherry schooner
coral islands in the Medway's qwag
peppermints dispensed by gloved hands
snuff on a spinnaker
unhurried asbestos to lace the lungs
many golden cuirasses of oilseed rape &
2 women with the initials 'JC'

pylon wires trench the land
kneejerk coloureds in the classroom
boat-hats & starfish pastries
drink up you lads at the sunset bar
punish mulattos & mestizas
whose children fly the coop unable to face
the rented grandiloquence of brazen crofts

ocean estate

fording pondlife to pamper your Arab steed
rosettes displayed above pillows
of cleanest straw – can't call
a whippet a dog (it's a bitch anyway &
hot enough to smear my shiny strides)
call it: longterm rewards of academic life

all the blood fruit wine that
flatters & does not grind the loaf you
squeeze cutting a pinbone pet
who has mislaid her bell

'forest' is no threat so much green
stacked until you close out
the other stuff the bearded
litigant poets incubating harm (despoiling
place) too pedigree'd to fart in tune

poets outgun symposium novelists
having less to say & saying it
with more conviction & smelling
like they *live* by choice in mismatched
suits (obligated to Burton's black)

the fust of old books & older cheese
nobody loves gossip like these salaried dudes

above us hangs a carmine cloud
the amputated leg of Harry Crews
stern invoice of what a writer's career
should entail – no kids & a drawerful of
biro caps to clean the wax from your ears

granted, all dream
but some of you, having better manners,
would never admit so much

Sussex
4 May 1995

bunhill fields

Secretly, he loved poetry.
– Tim Hilton (on Clement Greenberg)

the proximate fig shades a shale envelope
writing I have no intention of writing about this
heavy leaves green fed with grey fed up
between showers with being noticed shadows
where William & Catherine lie loose disinterred
a glazed brown pot in clay dead flowerheads
flower-smelling water incoherent autumn
sunlight free-associating through stone flags when
the blonde child on her precocious red bicycle
what did you say these were called again what
did you say *figs* figs figs but do they have seeds
confirmation speeds her certain way
balanced five-in-hand that might have ripened
juice on the vertical slab unsteady from wine lunch
a mossy cushion obelisks & peeled plaster faces
scarlet seeds on a thick black tongue

landschaft

no camera gun so the rain slides unthinking
rapturous from glass & by arrangement
into a stone basin where it can recover its poise
lie still the light is green as polyester cooler
than you'd expect of a sanctioned hothouse

imagined snakes press against the cloth of your coat
facing behind the century plant warm earth
that breathes faster than an hour in the gym
flowers & fades while the need remains
bands of perfume charge us we lack for sound

a raised dome becoming a machine should
cast its own portrait baguettes denied postscript
to hermit art primitive reds & greens tortures
of delight naked bodies writhing on the spike
the Jews Mound map deeded not to touch

all we own 31,936 km a walk around the world
true Spandau ballet danced in a cell a tv weather
voyage filmed in a Beirut cellar the last 12 years
imprisonment are the worst words held too long
in the mouth Listerine no substitute for speed

shirt off the rest to follow coming close to admitting
an automobile surprised by the mirror of other
poets paired dead calm & restless bladder stretched
'her teeth' the precise route to annul the mind
shapes a rock sand graves a 4-post yell – *o yes!* (& how)

Oxford
4 September 1995

the exhibition i didn't hold at the tate would have included

(1) ½ the pickled brain of Wyndham Lewis
(2) the mantle of Powhatan
(3) the Tradescants' missing Ark
(4) the skin of Ld Archer's back (with its prophetic moles)
(5) a silent video of JH Prynne's famous lecture on
     Willem de Kooning's *Rosy-Fingered Dawn at Louse Point*
(6) Jeremy Bentham mummified in a perspex Panopticon
(7) the River Thames

e/meth

'the sun our plant'

tolerance of hot monkey light
exposes the conservatory
as an arriviste sham

glove-throat laced to creak
waxed moustaches tickle the crease of your arm
hair mouth to prick of saddle soap

fissure of slender desire
a lingerie of hypertext to float

othering the angels

for David & Judy Gascoyne

comestible sunlight refined by the cherry tree's lush
machinery, October on the island
a lucky limbo & unearned audience with a perky revenant,
Chris Petit's Sharp freezing the moment's fan
to disclose the Terror of Europe, chocolate stealth, leafjig hair
or, anecdotes of Dr Bluth, Conrad Veidt, Anna Kavan
an armful of ox blood & Methedrine before the royal blue taxi
skids to a halt at the palace gates:
'do you realize sir this land is reborn? Jerusalem & all her angels?'

granite segments of fruit cake splinter a floral plate
resinous waves over the dancing table, murmurs
of parchment & ancient photographs packed like Egyptian
leaves under sticky laminate – Chairman Ginsberg in New York,
Robert Duncan wall-eyed in San Francisco, future memories
hoarded, journals recovered, get it over before it all happens again

the director's caramel Merc plainsman shirt £300 reduced
leather jacket from Harrods justifies a silent movie
'nearly as good, almost the same' the poet says, reliving
conversations from an abandoned book, sliding upstairs
in his throne to the tick of an insulated book-lined room

ivy on the rim. 'welcome' on blackboard at the door
french lessons in the window convex mirror
sunset over a milk shore. prisoners issued with acrylic
pencils. the daily poem. 'residual hope'

belhaven

rasp with tongue the belly of an old wristwatch
whip your swift tongue around my wrist
smell like New York Times Square
like spit chickens hotly
protesting their kerosene butter slaughter, or
a black girl in leather with a fur collar
stepping from the kerb at the junction of Restaurant Row
(where *Cats* is performed between bites) whispering
(no emphasis) 'wanna blow job?'
'what?' I say & she, undismayed, repeats it

the Paramount Hotel is underwater
drowned by Scientology coffee
made of dirt washed from Moloch gutters
yellow cabs illiterate between museums
Huncke's hutch Corso's clothes-strewn cabin
'hey man, don't take your shoes off'
til you know what Webster's dictionary means
by 'scryer' & Ed Sanders conducts the choir in a cold church
the heroically unlaved Mekas whacked by cinema

a gerontocracy of privileged ghosts
preserved in close rooms
views of an indifferent city
memory criminals repeating a fortune cookie mantra

snow-blocks to wind on the river
banished smoke across Mafia bones
buried cock-in-mouth, industrial
deadlands where bright planes queue for their winter enema

snow lip

For forgery, once, in Rutlandshire.
               – Angela Carter

bird-creole or the billowing froth of bride song
privately spoken & since unheard
from antechamber & dubious balcony caught
in bloody dew by the sheet-examiners, rare
music to the sweaty hair-man who excuses himself
to boast piss & dip his scalded organ
in the athanor's cruel furnace

overlook a vitreous pier beyond which
the sea is hard as remembered fire
curvature like the arm of an handless groom who
reaches across the alabaster pillow & cries
'touch me for our saviour's sake', kicks against
the lion stool that anchors his fretful sole

willing or not, the lake is artificial (as is her eye)
patterns of random magnetism
deform the church tower shattered by chopper blades
a showy landing in the wrong field:
mortal diners lay aside their forks, await measurement
white suits & parasols, not grasping what *that* portends

housewives juggle table plates
disguise penile shavings of pink fish-fruit
bile grapes & meat-ripe droppings,
take silver spoon & scoop the dripping clag of ash
into the infanta's generous bodice, manhandle fur

'nothing phases the river' he moans
drowning in his liar's blackened teeth

world's oldest comedian is dead

Barbers are murdered in the night!
         – Gregory Corso

walking through wet wheat an ocean of mercury after
the storm's head had snapped in the wound a
blunt spike driven deep into brain jelly – geography
of desire, sperm-tails photographed as galactic reductions
fetishes & footsore hyphens, delightful shoes,
neck-braces & mandrakes preserved in smoky bottles
disengage, alchemy & the alchemist, red sand – Russian
in name only, sour silk drenched under coarse
serge, Comrade Commissar, 'give us a twirl'
vile officer-class peons with cowshit on their boots
perform in flawless French while swilling
wineglasses whole, best red, *fin* on the broad screen
a word not a bite, a signal to pull back that ungloved hand
from its almond-oil trespass, the tongue from the cheek.
it spells refreshed light outside the fire door shaken
into coats, rain stalled, horn buttons undone
a loose belt, odd legs negotiating the cobbled slope
beneath an undistinguished church – a shark
in the shallows of a coffee-shop, mirrors everywhere
new underwear discreetly disclosed before it is discovered
(& distressed), another disappointing rhubarb *brûlée*
as preamble to permitted violation, the ghost of a girl
in the doorway of a small hotel, thanking us
for not contributing to her relief, the cocky Irishman
scoring a quid, hard coin, at the traffic lights
heraldic spoon twirling the coffee rust to glacial sand
'my ignorance has been well preserved'

revenge, laughter, paradise

saved in salt, face partially crushed & drooping eye
scalds egg from its skin in an over-occupied bedsit
(dig the view) book altar
occulted between shewstone & black candles
(fuck my glove) or check your ruin in an Aztec
obsidian mirror, set sail for fever islands on
a ticking couch, graceless garden plot, no
storyline (excess of script), palsy your pen pal, history is
the piss mark on an overnight bottle (analgesic gum
tongued from throat to kidney dish of purest crystal)

Kelley's retrieved fluid as a tripod globe
blood ink autumnal
felicitates the storm, an invitation
the grail cup
plays back in flawless gold

books made holy by inscription, or vandalized by those
who assert an author's rite she can't
end it with 'semen on his chin', sodden queen
presses lipstick over marble
Stergene unknown to her, trilobyte domestica
gives head on the floor on the wigs & the feathers, not
with a running tap & a blind voyeur in attendance
ganging up against the dead photographs
mouths silted in fearful intelligence

deluded curtains set in paint to open graciously
the evidence of a suicide leap confuses the scene
'the question that sticks in my throat'
no room this in which to imagine what might happen next

Acknowledgements

The poems in this selection are taken from the following books, to whose publishers acknowledgement is made: *Three Variations on the Theme of Harm: Selected Fiction and Poetry* (Paladin, 1990) and *Selected Poems* (Talisman House, NJ, 1996) for Douglas Oliver; *Mop Mop Georgette, New and Selected Poems 1986–1993* (Reality Street Editions, 1993) for Denise Riley; *Flesh Eggs & Scalp Metal* (Hoarse Commerce, 1983), *Autistic Poses* (Hoarse Commerce, 1985), *Significant Wreckage* (Words Press, 1988), *Flesh Eggs & Scalp Metal: Selected Poems 1970–1987* (Paladin, 1989) and *Jack Elam's Other Eye* (Hoarse Commerce, 1991) for Iain Sinclair.